Teacher's Manual

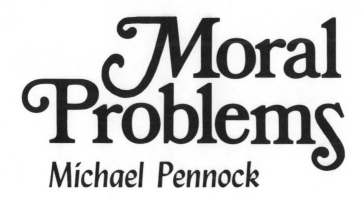

# Moral Problems

Michael Pennock

Ave María Press • Notre Dame, Ind. 46556

# Contents

# Introduction

My purpose here is to orient you to the Teacher's Manual for the text *Moral Problems: What Does a Christian Do?* But before I proceed, I wish to thank you for selecting the text and teaching it to your students.

I want to dedicate this manual to you, my fellow laborers in the Lord. I pray that the Lord continues to bless you and your work and that he will inspire your students to live the Christian life.

## WHY THIS BOOK?

Several things prompted me to write this book. First, I have found that my students need more than just a knowledge of the principles of Christian morality such as are presented in *Christian Morality and You*. Principles need to be applied in order to have any practical value. My years of teaching have shown me that high school students have great difficulty in systematically discussing and thinking through moral issues. The work of Daniel Maguire, Charles Curran, Richard McCormick, William May and other leading Catholic moralists has demonstrated that clear thinking and a method of moral analysis is absolutely necessary to treat moral issues *intelligently.* Borrowing heavily from these, especially Prof. Maguire, I have devised a method that has been successful in helping young people analyze moral cases.

A second reason I wrote this book is that young people genuinely enjoy discussing moral issues, but there is a dearth of material available for them.

Finally, I wrote this book because I thoroughly enjoy the field. It is an exciting topic because it is so practical in living the Christian life of response to God's love. It was a fun book to research and to pilot. I am honored to share it with you.

## MY PHILOSOPHY

The text was written with a number of assumptions on my part. I want to share these with you.

*Young people need a systematic approach to solve moral problems.* I am of the old school that believes "grace builds on nature." Also, I have conducted too many class discussions which seemingly went in all directions, ending up nowhere. I am convinced that Christian decision-making, like all decision-making, does not necessarily have to happen haphazardly. Students need to see that right behavior, moral choice, is not accidental. A lot of hard work goes into living the Christian life. At the basis of this hard work are a number of questions that must be asked. An integral part of human nature is to ask questions intelligently and to know where to get answers. The method presented in the text is a systematic way of asking many of the important questions that need to be asked about moral issues.

*Jesus is the objective norm of morality.* If you are familiar with the theological literature, you will notice that I was inspired in the first few chapters by the thought of the Catholic ethician, Daniel Maguire. About half of the elements in my method come from his insights as discussed most recently in his book, *The Moral Choice.* However, what is

lacking in an *ethical* approach to moral questions is the role
of Jesus. I am absolutely convinced that at the heart of Catholic morality is Jesus who is our norm for doing the right
thing. His teaching has a central place in any approach to
moral decision-making in the Christian tradition. Furthermore, he must be offered to our students as a personal Savior
who can help them in their moral decisions. Consequently,
prayer is treated as an important means of contacting the risen
Lord who is vitally interested in his brothers and sisters on
their way to the Father. Also, his abiding presence in the
Christian community, that is, fellow believers, and in the
teaching authority of the church must be presented to students as important ways to follow the Lord. These are over-
riding themes that are continuously treated in the method of
discovering the right thing to do.

*The Catholic tradition is a source of pride in studying
moral issues.* The more I study moral theology, the more I
am convinced that our Catholic tradition is a rich source for
working out moral problems. From the word of God in the
New Testament through the Second Vatican Council to the
work of creative moral theologians of contemporary times,
young people should be given the opportunity to appreciate
their spiritual and intellectual roots. I believe it is valuable
for them to see the richness of our tradition. It is not that
we as teachers are to picture the church in a triumphalistic
way, assuming that we have all the answers. Rather, it is
that the church's long tradition has done a considerable
service in asking the right questions. These questions and
the creative responses to them cannot be ignored.

*Modern psychological insights are helpful in our task
of catechizing.* If it is true that grace builds on nature, then
it is helpful for us as religious educators to know what contemporary social scientists are saying about the young people
we teach. The research of developmental psychologists like
Jean Piaget and Lawrence Kohlberg is helpful in learning
about young people. The work of James Fowler is valuable
in the area of faith development. There is no need to canonize
these thinkers; their work is still in progress. But they can
help us in our presentation of moral problems.

Kohlberg, especially, has shown rather convincingly that discussion of moral dilemmas is an effective way for students to see moral issues from more sophisticated levels. My own teaching experience also demonstrates that this is true. Group discussion is a form of peer education—a very valuable form of education. I have included a number of cases that should be thoroughly discussed in order for them to have their full impact. Values education is also a worthwhile tool in teaching morality. Although I strongly believe that Catholic religious educators have the duty to challenge certain values held by students, I further believe that the techniques of the values clarification revolution are very helpful in initiating thought and discussion. I include many of these techniques in the text.

*There is no one way to teach morality or to tackle moral issues.* Even though I present a method of approaching and solving moral issues, I believe that adaptability ought to be the keyword for moral educators. I encourage you to picture the text as a tool, a jumping-off point for beginning your own discussions and examinations of moral issues. To this end, I include a number of references throughout this manual which will help you adapt the material to your own teaching style and your own students.

## CURRICULUM PLAN OF THE BOOK

A systems analysis approach to the text will reveal the following about it.*

*Objectives:* The main objectives of the text are as follows:

1. That students are able to define morality.
2. That students can apply critically the method of moral analysis presented in the text to a number of moral issues, cases and problems.
3. That students reflect on their own values in light of church teaching and various other contemporary ethical philosophies.

4. That students are able to discuss sexual morality in light of the moral method studied in the text.

5. That students show facility in evaluating various contemporary ethical positions on abortion.

6. That students be able to articulate the church's teaching on sin.

7. That students demonstrate an ability to research a moral issue, especially in the areas of life, truth and justice.

8. That students are able to recognize various stages of moral growth and development.

These eight objectives are the major unifying objectives of the text. Each chapter, however, has a number of subsidiary objectives. Each of these will be stated in this Teacher's Manual in the chapters following.

*Content:* The content of the book is both cognitive and affective. The major cognitive content of the book includes a discussion of the 12 points of the moral method known as the STOP sign, a definition of morality, sexual morality, abortion in a pluralistic context, sin, life issues, truth and justice issues and moral decision-making. Affective content consists of a number of exercises that attempt to get students to question, reflect, value, choose and internalize their own morality. Several points in the STOP sign method are affective outcomes that request students to imagine, to trust their feelings and to follow their consciences. There are no explicit psychomotor contents although several of the action projects may be approaching such a content.

*Scope:* The scope of the book is limited to mastery of the STOP sign method of moral analysis, and a discussion of several key themes in Catholic morality such as sex, abortion, sin, life, truth and justice and a definition of morality. A

_____

* I am indebted to Dr. Larry Bradley, Ph.D., for his clear articulation of this curriculum approach.

theoretical discussion of many contemporary moral issues is avoided. Rather, the approach is quite practical and limited to problems and cases which students can wrestle with from their own experience and the data provided in the text. Several chapters, however, do encourage students to broaden their study by further research. In all cases, sufficient resources are given so that students have clear guidance on where to begin researching issues. Around 30 cases and an equal number of values exercises are included for students to apply the principles they learned. Numerous discussion questions are sprinkled throughout the book.

*Sequence and Content Organization of the Chapters:*

Chapter 1: Introduction

1. Life involves morality
2. Various ethical positions
3. Overview of book
4. Three definitions of morality
5. A key case for discussion: lifeboat ethics

Chapter 2: The "STOP" Sign

1. Search out the facts: What, Why, Who, When, Where, How
2. Think about the consequences and the alternatives
3. Others—consider them and consult them
4. Pray

Chapter 3: The STOP Sign, Continued

1. The dimension of Jesus in morality
2. Reason and revelation
3. Imagination
4. Law—principles and authority

Chapter 4: The STOP Sign, Concluded

1. Church
2. Values
3. Instinct
4. Conscience

Chapter 5: The STOP Sign Applied

Premarital sexual morality discussed in light of the STOP sign

Chapter 6: Moral Pluralism

1. An ethical debate on abortion
2. Analysis of the debate
3. Abortion reconsidered

Chapter 7: Morality and Sin

1. Talk about sin
2. Sinning as saying "no"
3. Jesus and forgiveness

Chapter 8: Solving Moral Problems: What about Life?

1. Background on life
2. Some cases on life issues
3. Data on euthanasia
4. Data on capital punishment

Chapter 9: Solving Moral Problems: Truth and Justice

1. What is honesty?
2. What is justice?
3. Some cases for discussion
4. Appendix on justice, including activities

Chapter 10: Reasoning Morally and Conclusion

1. Kohlberg's six stages
2. Some more cases
3. Quiz on book

It is essential that the first four chapters be taught in order. They introduce the topics of the book and detail the STOP sign method of moral decision-making. Chapter 5 follows logically from the first four in that it demonstrates how the method is applied to a single moral issue. But you may wish to take any other case from the last three chapters or the one from Chapter 6 to illustrate the method. It is not essential to take any of the other chapters in order, although

I have found it very helpful to discuss the issue of moral pluralism and the topic of sin before delving into the other cases. However, you may wish to treat sin as the final topic in the book. Nevertheless, the evaluative quiz at the end of Chapter 10 assumes that all the topics in the book have already been treated. None of the cases in Chapters 8, 9 and 10 need to be discussed in any particular order.

*Method and Media:* After a presentation of the material, you will find that the major method of the book is discussion and sharing. This follows from my conviction discussed in Chapter 2 of the text that others can be a great help in solving moral issues. Another major technique employed in meeting the objectives is various kinds of values clarification exercises. Finally, the text leaves room for individual research and group projects of various kinds as a valuable way to learn morality. Although I do not make explicit reference to any media in the text itself, films and filmstrips that may be used in various ways are recommended in this manual. I have used film extensively in my teaching of morality; it is a rich source of case material and has a way of engaging students' hearts as well as their minds.

*Evaluation:* The quiz at the end of the book may be used as a measure of how well students have grasped the cognitive objectives of the text. Page numbers of correct answers are provided so that students can study those sections which need review. Also, cases may be used as a way to evaluate how well students apply the various elements of the STOP sign. These may be drawn from almost any chapter of the book.

## ESSENTIAL TEACHER READING

It is impossible to list and discuss even a small sample of the many rich books available to the teacher of morality. Here I will list and briefly annotate those which I find to be extremely useful. In each chapter of the Teacher's Manual I will list and annotate many other books that can help you present the material in the text.

Bockle, Franz. *Fundamental Concepts of Moral Theology.* New York: Paulist Press, 1968. A clear, traditional presentation of Catholic moral theology, including many of the basic concepts discussed in the text. Excellent background reading.

Duska, Ronald and Mariellen Whelan. *Moral Development: A Guide to Piaget and Kohlberg.* New York: Paulist Press, 1975. Excellent introduction to both Piaget and Kohlberg. A definite contribution to understanding the moral development of our students.

Dunning, James B. *Values in Conflict: A Christian Approach to Decision Making.* Cincinnati: Pflaum, 1976. Includes some useful exercises and a helpful approach to making moral decisions. An easy book to read. Dunning was also influenced by Maguire.

Finley, James and Michael Pennock. *Christian Morality and You: Right and Wrong in an Age of Freedom.* Notre Dame, Indiana: Ave Marie Press, 1976. Our text on principles of Christian morality. Good teacher background reading.

Hennessy, S.J., Thomas C., ed. *Values and Moral Development.* New York: Paulist Press, 1976. Contains some excellent articles by major thinkers in moral development. Most valuable are the critical essays on the articles. Must reading.

Kee, Howard Clark. *Making Ethical Decisions.* Philadelphia: The Westminister Press, 1957. This might be a difficult book to locate but it is well worth the hunt. The author writes from the Protestant tradition. He gives some excellent approaches to solving moral issues and includes a number of provocative cases.

Maguire, Daniel C. *The Moral Choice.* Garden City, New York: Doubleday & Company, Inc., 1978. I cannot recommend better reading for you. Though he writes ethical philosophy, Maguire is simply outstanding. His method is without parallel and greatly influenced the approach I took in writing the text.

Mattox, Beverly A. *Getting It Together: Dilemmas for the Classroom.* San Diego: Pennant Press, 1975. Gives many useful dilemmas suitable for high school classroom discussion.

*Moral Education and Christian Conscience: Value Education in Perspective.* Washington, D.C.: United States Catholic Conference, 1977. Contains very good essays on conscience and theories of moral development, as well as educational guidelines in moral education.

McNulty, Frank J. *Invitation to Greatness.* Denville, New Jersey: Dimension Books, 1974. McNulty writes simply and sees morality as joyous. A nice book to get you enthused about teaching morality to young people.

Regan, C.M., George M. *New Trends in Moral Theology.* New York: Newman Press, 1971. An outstanding overview of Catholic moral theology in the post-Vatican II Church. The bibliographies alone are worth pursuing the book.

Savary, Louis M. *Integrating Values.* Dayton, Ohio: Pflaum, 1974. Uses Lonergan's decision-making process and applies it to value development. An interesting approach that will give you many ideas for student journal-keeping.

Sloyan, Gerard S. *How Do I Know I'm Doing Right?* New York: Pflaum, 1976. An outstanding, simple introduction to Christian morality. You must read this book because it will give you a marvelous scriptural basis to a number of themes presented in the student text.

Sullivan, Edmund V. *Moral Learning: Findings, Issues, and Questions.* New York: Paulist Press, 1975. A statistically based analysis of moral education experiments of elementary and secondary school students. Helps you to know where students are in their moral development.

Scharf, Peter, ed. *Readings in Moral Education.* Minneapolis: Winston Press, 1978. The best collection of readings on moral education that I have found. Many practical ideas will flow from a careful reading of this text.

## STRUCTURE OF THE TEACHER'S MANUAL

Each chapter of the Teacher's Manual contains the following sections.

*Background:* This is an orientation to the chapter. I try to give a bird's-eye view of the content and discuss the significance of the theological theme treated.

*Further Reading for the Teacher:* Included here are selected readings that helped me in my research. I will annotate each resource and key in on those chapters that are especially valuable for the presentation of the material in a given chapter of the text. Except in rare cases, I will not repeat works from chapter to chapter, thus giving you a rather extensive bibliography of works that can be most helpful for your own background in moral theology. Most of the works cited are readily available and have tended to receive good reviews in the professional journals. The bibliographies in Chapters 6, 8 and 9 of the student text are also valuable teacher references.

*Objectives:* Chapters vary in the number of objectives stated, but in most cases there are five to seven of them. Where possible, objectives will be stated in behavioral terms but many of them are necessarily unobservable in terms of measurable behaviors. These latter objectives are more aptly termed *expressive* objectives in that they describe an educational encounter that is *evocative* rather than prescriptive. These latter objectives, especially in the affective domain, allow students to explore, defer and focus.

*Procedure:* A suggested step-by-step procedure is provided for presentation of the material in the chapter. In some cases, I will offer some more doctrinal background to help you in elucidating the text. On occasion, I will give an exercise or two not included in the text. Within the various steps, you may find alternative procedures suggested. The steps will often suggest particular audio-visual resources that I have found useful in my own teaching. The references for these and alternative audio-visuals are treated in the subsequent section of the Teacher's Manual ("Suggested Audiovisual Ideas").

Within the text itself, I tried not to present more than two or three pages of development without a break of some kind, allowing students to pause and apply what they have learned. I strongly recommend that the cases, values exercises and discussion questions not be skimmed over. In many ways, they represent the flesh of the text and can heighten student attention and interest in the material presented. The cases especially ask students to apply, analyze, synthesize and evaluate—the higher levels of cognitive learning.

*Suggested Audiovisual Ideas:* Included here are audiovisual resources with which I am familiar or have used successfully with my own students either in the Catholic high school or CCD setting. I highly encourage you to supplement the text with liberal use of these. They have the benefit of giving the students a common experience and help engage their feelings as well as their intellects. Addresses where these resources can be rented or purchased are listed at the end of the manual.

*Time Used:* Based on my own use of these materials, I try to suggest how long (or short) each step takes. I assume at least a 40- to 50-minute period. You can comfortably teach this book in one semester if you meet every day. I have also taught it in one quarter but had to be selective in what I emphasized. Student research projects alone can be quite time-consuming, especially if you allow students to give oral presentations. Obviously, these times will vary a great deal depending on what you intend to emphasize.

*CCD Adaptation:* I have taught the meat of the text to high school CCD students for the equivalent of a 10-hour minicourse. Using the text and especially the exercises as a base, I will show you how the book can be used in a student-centered, discussion-format CCD setting. My assumption for the successful presentation of the text's material to CCD students is that the teacher is very familiar with the student text and the contents of the "Procedure" sections of the Teacher's Manual. This familiarity will enable you to field most student questions and will allow you to lead better discussions.

# 1

## Introduction: Getting Started

### BACKGROUND

The student text begins with an introduction to the topic of morality in general. It tries to show that all of life involves morality. After this brief introduction, an important exercise is presented in order to stress that, depending on one's philosophy of life, a person will tend to judge issues differently. The exercise is explained by reference to the major moral positions held by people in the Western world.

After an overview of the book, three different definitions of morality are given. Although the text does not discuss the issue, morality is presented as a different concept than ethics. The definitions presented are from Catholic thinkers. The terms *moral, immoral* and *amoral* are distinguished. The chapter ends with an extremely important case on lifeboat ethics. This case will appear in the subsequent three chapters as students will be asked to apply various elements of the **STOP** sign to it.

You may find the supplementary information discussed below valuable to present to the students. It is worth the effort to distinguish "Christian morality" from "ethics." Also, you may wish to discuss the term "new morality." Students run into these terms in the literature and it may be worthwhile for you to define them at the beginning of their study of morality and moral problems.

### SUPPLEMENT: What is ethics?

One definition of ethics is that it is the study of standards for human conduct *using human reason alone*. It is the search in light of human intelligence to come up with certain norms of behavior. All societies have developed some kind of ethical wisdom to help members in the society to live and to guide their behavior according to acceptable norms. By using reason alone, very few societies have developed ethics which are exactly alike. For example, the standards of human life for the aborigines of Australia are quite different from those of Soviet Russia. Likewise, the ethics of ancient Rome were dissimilar to the code of conduct of the Vandals who attacked the limits of the Empire.

Because ethical behavior, what is considered right and wrong, varies from culture to culture, some have said that all ethics is relative. What is meant by the relative nature of ethics is that you cannot say any behavior or attitude is *the* right or wrong behavior or attitude. It all depends on the society in which you live. What is right for an aborigine might be wrong for a Russian and vice versa. For example, take the following case: What would be your reaction to a 12-year-old boy who was challenged to a footrace but refused to run? His friends tease him and mock him. They try to provoke him and urge him on. As an American you might say that the boy would do one of two things: either take up the challenge or fight to defend his honor. In contemporary American society, competition is highly valued. Not to compete is to go against the prevailing custom. But if the boy in the story were a Navaho Indian, he would simply walk away. There would be no shame in refusing to run because, for the Navaho, competition is not highly prized.

This example points to the relative nature of ethics: what is considered right or wrong greatly varies from society to society, from one historical period to the next. If this is true, it leaves us with a dilemma: Is nothing ever considered wrong? Have men and women in all places at all times not been able to come up with certain behaviors that are always considered right or wrong no matter what? Cultural anthropologists, those who compare and contrast cultures, do tell us that there are wide differences among cultures and ages. However, there are many similarities as well, like respect for human life, a sense of justice, a concern for social order. It is almost certain that every society has condemned cold-blooded murder. The calculated taking of the life of an innocent person without just cause has been universally condemned because it is so destructive that if it were tolerated, the society itself would crumble.

Rape also seems to be one of those actions which are rarely, if ever, tolerated within a society. Why? Human reason dictates that rape is so destructive of what it means to be human, that it tears at the heart of society by destroying trust and harmonious relationships, that it cannot be considered right behavior. Finally, cultural anthropologists sometimes mention blasphemy as a universal taboo in societies. Blasphemy is defined as cursing of the deity, whatever one might consider the god to be. Thus, for example, an aborigine would not tolerate the cursing of the rain god; the loyal communist would not allow bad-mouthing of the communist party or one of its heroes such as Karl Marx; the Moslem would condemn anyone who profanes the name of Allah.

Beyond these, there are few examples cultural anthropologists can point to in order to show that human reason has discovered certain actions and attitudes that are always right or wrong. They would say that if you want to solve moral problems, you have to enter a particular society, become a member of it, learn its ethics, and then settle your problem. All of ethics is pretty much relative in this view. For the Christian, the way out of this dilemma is to go beyond ethics to morality because morality adds an extremely important dimension to any discussion of right and wrong.

*SUPPLEMENT: The "new morality"*

Play a word-association game with someone over the age of 28 or so. Ask the person to say the first thing that comes to mind when he or she hears the term "the new morality." Then, ask the person if the thing or concept that came to mind has a positive, negative or neutral connotation. You may be surprised at your findings. For many people, the so-called "new morality" has many negative overtones. They often think of sexual promiscuity and the bad effects of the cultural revolution that came about in the 1960's and 1970's. Certainly, the news media has used the phrase "the new morality" this way. For example, a recent news item told of a young college man who lived in a dormitory. For a fee he would answer the telephone for fellow students whenever their parents called them. He would tell the parents that their son was out, probably studying in the library. Then, he would inform his classmate that his parents had called and to return the call. In reality the son was living in an off-campus apartment with a coed. The news item described this enterprising young man as a product of the new morality that advocates premarital sex. Critics of the new morality say that it is merely old immorality dressed up in new clothes.

However, some scholars have noted that the phrase "the new morality" should be taken in a positive sense with the emphasis placed on the words freedom, love and responsibility. They point to some positive changes that have been made in the study of morality in the past 20 years or so, changes that try to get away from rigid rules and regulations that can and sometimes do dehumanize people who are called to be responsible. They see the break from rigid authority as a good, not a bad thing.

Because of the confusion and emotion connected with the so-called new morality, the student text will avoid using that term. Rather, it will attempt to present Christian morality in a post-Vatican II Catholic Church.

## FURTHER READING FOR THE TEACHER

Baum, Robert and James Randell, eds. *Ethical Arguments for Analysis.* New York: Holt, Rinehart and Winston, Inc., 1973. An excellent resource for cases and various views on the same topic. A top-notch supplement for a course in moral problems.

Bender, David L. *Constructing a Life Philosophy: An Examination of Alternatives.* Anoka, Minnesota: Greenhaven Press, Inc., 1976. A student text that is loaded with readings and exercises on different life philosophies. Many ethical issues raised. Must reading.

Curran, Charles E. *Christian Morality Today.* Notre Dame, Indiana: Fides Publishers, Inc., 1966. Chapter 8 discusses the relevance of moral theology today.

Curran, Charles E. *Ongoing Revision in Moral Theology.* Notre Dame, Indiana: Fides Publishers, Inc., 1975. The first chapter discusses the difference between Catholic, Christian and human ethics. Good distinctions drawn.

Frankl, Viktor. *Man's Search for Meaning.* New York: Pocket Books, 1971. A classic book that dramatically points out how one's philosophy affects one's life, especially in the most dire circumstances. This would be good student reading, too.

Lohkamp, O.F.M., Nicholas. *What's Happening to Morality?* Cincinnati: St. Anthony Messenger Press, 1971. An easy introduction to the new emphases in Catholic morality. Very positive in tone.

Oraison, Marc. *Morality for Our Time.* Garden City, New
York: Image Books, 1968. Discusses in depth Sertil-
langes' definition of morality. Stresses freedom and
responsibility in morality. Good reading.

OBJECTIVES

That the student . . .

1. *Recognize* that all of life involves morality.

2. *Differentiate* between the major ethical systems in
   contemporary society.

3. *Decide* from a number of situations what is right or
   wrong.

4. *Define* morality.

5. *Distinguish* between the terms *moral, immoral* and
   *amoral.*

6. *Discuss* intelligently a case in lifeboat ethics.

7. (Optional) *Characterize* ethics as distinct from
   morality.

PROCEDURE

*Step 1:* Read together page 9. Discuss the question on the
top of page 10.

*Step 2:* Summarize the introduction to the exercise on page
10. Have students do the exercise on page 10. Discuss
the questions on page 12.

*Alternative:* Allow students to order these five philosophies according to what they think is most prevalent
in America to the least prevalent. As a class, write
two or three more statements to add to the list. Later,
try to identify these according to the scheme on page
12.

*Step 3:* Look at plan of the book on page 13. Briefly explain
what each element in the *STOP* sign refers to.

*Step 4:* (Optional) From the supplement entitled "What is ethics?"—give a short presentation citing the relativity of ethics. Use this as a lead-in to the exercise on page 16.

*Step 5:* Allow students time to fill in the exercise on page 16. Take time to discuss the questions at the end of the exercise.

    a. Analyze each item in terms of the five ethical positions discussed on page 12. Some of the items have more than one possible philosophy behind them—this is fine. Your only objective here is to get students to think in terms of them.

    b. *Alternative:* Show and discuss the short film entitled *Inscape* or the filmstrip *Man Today.* (See some suggested alternatives in the Audiovisual section.) These both raise some interesting points of value discussion for young people and help achieve the same goal as the exercise.

*Step 6:* Definitions of morality, pages 18-23.
In discussing the important points of these definitions of morality, be sure to stress the following:

    a. *Without freedom there is no morality.* (Here, ask students to give examples of license—unbridled freedom—in order to distinguish it from true freedom.)

    b. *Morality is guided by revelation.* (Here, elicit some norms students live by because of revelation. This will help you see how much they already know about revelation, an important element in the STOP sign.)

    c. *Morality is a science.* (You may want to distinguish between physical sciences and human sciences. In the latter case, human existence has an unpredictable element in it—we are mysterious. We can continuously grow in living better lives of response to others as we learn more about ourselves.)

d. *Morality judges in light of what man is.* (Here, have students survey a number of magazines, newspapers and TV shows. Let them select advertisements that depict humans in a mechanistic or self-indulgent way. Share the ads and ask how the underlying philosophy behind them would have people act in a situation that would call for self-sacrifice. As an alternative to this, discuss the five most popular TV shows and the philosophy of humans underlying them.)

e. *Morality is responsibility.* (Ignace Lepp claims in his *The Authentic Morality* that Christian morality can be defined as responding to the needs of others. This makes sense in light of the fact that Jesus coupled love of God with love of neighbor. You may wish to share this insight with your class.)

*Step 7:* (Optional) Ask students to write down the first thing that comes to mind when they hear the term "the new morality." Share these and discuss whether they have negative or positive connotations. Then, share some of the insights from the supplement entitled "The New Morality" from the background section. As a homework assignment, tell students to play the word-association game with a person over the age of 30. Have them report the results in a subsequent class.

*Step 8:* Read the "To think about" section on p. 23 and do the exercise at the end. Clearly explain the relationship between Christian and Catholic morality on pages 23-24.

*Step 9:* Summary.

*Step 10:* Discuss the case on page 25.

    a. Highly recommended is that you show the film cutting made from this case entitled *The Right to Live: Who Decides?* This 15-minute film is well worth the $25 rental fee because it thoroughly engages students in the case.

    b. You may want to use another film to introduce a case that will provide adequate meat for a sustained discussion over several chapters. To this end, I recommend *The Incident,* a full-length feature film (101 minutes). It tells the story of a couple of hoodlums who get on a subway train late at night in New York City and proceed to terrorize the people on the train. The passengers remain isolated from one another. The end presents a predictable violent act which may have been avoided. The point of the movie is that we are our brother's keeper. The film is an updated version of the Good Samaritan. I highly recommend it and have had much success with it over the years.

## SUGGESTED AUDIOVISUAL IDEAS

*Automania 2000* (10 min. color film; McGraw-Hill). An animated satire on how scientific progress tends to dehumanize us. (Step 2)

*But What If the Dream Comes True?* (52 min. color documentary; CBS film). A shocking documentary of the values of an affluent American family produced by Charles Kuralt. (Step 5)

*The Eye of the Beholder* (25 minute color film; BNA Communications). Good on showing how a person is perceived by others and how this shapes self-perception. (Step 4 )

*The Incident* (101 minute black and white feature film; Films, Inc.). An excellent modern-day Good Samaritan. Good for sustained discussion. Rents for around $65. (Step 10)

*Inscape* (28 min. color film; Teleketics). A couple of young people share their hang-ups about life in general. A good introduction to a search for values. (Step 5)

*Man Today* (2 part filmstrip; 15 min. each; Alpha Corporation). The first filmstrip asks the question, "Is there any meaning in life?" The second leaves the viewer with the notion that hope is possible when we look to nature, Christ and our fellow humans. (Step 5)

*Nuclear Dilemma* (40 min. color film produced by the BBC; Time-Life). Examines the energy crunch and the problems with nuclear energy as a potential solution to the problem. A good starter film to show the range of moral problems. (Step 1)

*Right to Live: Who Decides?* (15 min. black and white film; Learning Corporation of America). Presents the famous lifeboat ethics case from a film snippet of *Abandon Ship*. The most important film from this chapter. (Step 10)

*30 Second Dream* (15 min. color film; Mass Media Ministries). Depicts a number of TV ads and their message: One is inadequate as a person without buying these products. Shows how we are manipulated by the media. (Step 2 or Step 6)

## TIME USED

Class 1: Steps 1, 2 and 3
Class 2: Steps 4 and 5
Class 3: Step 5 (if a film is used)
Class 4: Step 6
Class 5: Steps 7, 8 and 9
Class 6: Step 10

*Additional classes:* add one if you show *The Right to Live: Who Decides?* or any of the other short films described above; add two to three if you decide to show *The Incident.*

## ADAPTATION FOR CCD CLASSES

You should have no trouble adapting this chapter to a one-hour CCD class. The assumption here is that you are very familiar with the contents of the student text and the procedure in the manual. If at all possible, try to show one of the short films referred to in the Audiovisual section to involve students immediately in the course. Here is a suggested procedure:

*Step 1:* (15 min.) Have students work on the exercise on pages 10-11. Discuss the questions on page 12. Briefly refer to the ethical positions on page 12.

*Step 2:* (20 min.) Do the exercise on pages 16-17, making sure that students discuss the questions on page 18. Use this as a lead-in to a definition of morality.

*Step 3:* (10 min.) Give a very short lecture trying to define morality. Stress the points discussed in the procedure, Step 6 above.

*Step 4:* (15 min.)

   a. Have students look at the STOP sign. Quickly explain what each element refers to.

   b. Begin discussion of the lifeboat case on page 25. Leave the solution open-ended so that you can come back to it next session.

# 2

# The "STOP" Sign

## BACKGROUND

This chapter begins the three-chapter explanation of the method for moral decision-making known as the STOP sign, an acronym for a major concept in the method. Each letter of the STOP sign is discussed and analyzed as well as applied to concrete cases and examples. Very briefly the letters refer to:

S—*Searching* out the facts in a case or problem: what, why, who, where, when, how.

T—*Thinking* about the alternatives to the proposed problem and the consequences that might be involved.

O—*Others* must come into play because our actions affect them. Also, we are social beings so it is important to consult others.

P—*Prayer* is an important dimension in Christian moral decision-making. It puts us in contact with the Risen Lord and his Spirit.

Each of the elements is discussed in turn; furthermore, students are asked to apply what they learned to the lifeboat case introduced in Chapter 1.

This chapter also treats a couple of important principles of traditional Catholic morality. These principles are: The end does not justify the means, and if any elements in the moral case are evil (the moral object—what is done; the motive; or the circumstances), the action itself should be considered wrong. Students are given some exercises in which they are asked to apply these two principles.

Two things are important to stress in this chapter. The first is that morality—that is, Christian living—takes work. Thought involves work; hence, the method itself implies that students be patient with themselves until they learn a way to attack moral issues and problems. Their patience will pay off in the long run because they will have learned a way to proceed in analyzing moral issues. The second thing to stress in this chapter is the central role of prayer in Christian decision-making. An assumption in the text is that *Christian* morality looks to Jesus as the absolute norm of Christian behavior. Unless students become aware of this truth and the importance of contacting him through prayer, the method might merely degenerate into an exercise in logic or a neat ethical approach to troublesome problems. From an early stage on, students should be invited to pray. The teacher's personal testimony on how prayer aided in solving one's own problems in life can go a long way to help make this very important section of the book credible.

## FURTHER READING FOR THE TEACHER

Bockle, Franz. *Fundamental Concepts of Moral Theology.* New York: Paulist Press, 1968. Chapter 2 is invaluable in discussing the sources of morality in traditional terms.

Dedek, John F. *Titius and Bertha Ride Again: Contemporary Moral Cases.* New York: Sheed and Ward, Inc., 1974. Fr. Dedek is one of the clearest writers around. You might enjoy his casuistry in working on several contemporary cases. Also, his method of presenting cases simply might give you some good ideas on how to write your own.

Hardon, S. J., John A. *The Catholic Catechism.* Garden City, New York: Doubleday & Company, Inc., 1975. Fr. Hardon's Chapter 9 on norms and postulates in morality gives an extremely clear and brief treatment of traditional principles of Catholic morality. Fr. Hardon knows the tradition well and can get to the heart of it.

Haring, Bernard. *The Law of Christ,* 3 vols. Paramus, New Jersey: Newman Press, 1961, 1963, 1966. This seminal trilogy of Haring's has gone a long way in renewing Catholic moral theology. A basic familiarity with these texts is an absolute necessity.

Maguire, Daniel C. *Contemporary Moral Problems.* Kansas City, Mo.: N.C.R. Cassettes, 1973. It is well worth purchasing this 22-lesson cassette course from Prof. Maguire. It contains his seminal thought later to be developed in *A Moral Choice.* He presents many interesting and amusing examples to illustrate his ethical method.

May, William E. *Becoming Human: An Invitation to Christian Ethics.* Dayton: Pflaum, 1975. Chapter 4 is especially relevant to the themes of this chapter. May is traditional but very balanced and convincing.

Salm, F.S.C., C. Luke. *Readings in Biblical Morality.* Englewood Cliffs, New Jersey: Prentice-Hall, Inc., 1967. Bernard Haring's article on prudence can help in case you wish to develop further the notion behind the quotes at the beginning of Chapters 1 and 2 of the student text.

Varga, Andrew C. *On Being Human: Principles of Ethics.* New York: Paulist Press, 1978. This entire book is excellent background and will give you a good introduction to Christian ethics. This is an easy book to read and would be excellent preparation to teaching Chapters 2 and 3 of the student text.

## OBJECTIVES

That the student . . .

1. *Recall* the steps involved in the S-T-O-P section of the STOP sign method of moral decision-making.

2. *Apply* the following questions to selected moral problems:
    a. What is involved in the problem?
    b. Why does the person act this way?
    c. Who is involved?
    d. Where and when is the action to take place?
    e. How is the action to be performed?
    f. What are the alternatives?
    g. What are the foreseeable consequences?
    h. How will the action affect others?
    i. Have others been consulted?
    j. Has prayer been considered?

3. *Analyze* certain issues in light of two principles of Catholic morality.

4. *Identify* various elements involved in moral cases according to the scheme of moral object, intention or circumstances.

5. *Evaluate* the Captain's behavior in light of the S-T-O-P section of the Stop sign.

6. *Appreciate* the role of prayer in moral decision-making.

## PROCEDURE

*Step 1:* Read the first two paragraphs of the chapter. Here are a couple of exercises you might engage in:

    a. Have students brainstorm a list of 10 routine decisions that demand little moral reasoning. List these on the board or overhead and then discuss whether any moral issue is involved in any of them.

b. Have each student list three daily decisions that clearly *do* involve a moral decision. Share these with the class.

*Step 2:* Summarize the main points of the *Search* as discussed in the text, pp. 22-33. Use some of the examples from the text or ones that you create to illustrate the application of the 5 *w's* and *h*.

a. Discuss thoroughly with the students the lifeboat case using the questions on p. 31, p. 34, and p. 35. You may do this either in a large group or by assigning various questions to smaller groups. If you assign to smaller groups, let them report back to the larger group for sharing.

b. Practice identifying the 5 *w's* and *h*. Suggestion: Bring to class multiple copies of news stories from daily newspapers or weekly newsmagazines. Read some of the lead stories and pick out the various elements of the *Search* procedure. Some of the stories you find may very well lend themselves to more detailed discussion as well. (By the way, it is good early on in the course to alert students to look for moral cases in the news media. You may wish to make each student responsible for finding and bringing to class five or six articles that lend themselves to discussion. Make this assignment early in the course and you will have a rich source of cases for discussion throughout the course.)

c. Do the exercises on p. 38. Clearly reexplain the principle: "The end does not justify the means" before doing exercise #2. The following items deserve a check mark: a, c, e, f, h.

*Step 3:* Clearly explain the principle discussed on p. 39. Do the exercises on p. 40. My choices for the items in the exercise are as follows: 1. why; 2. where; 3. what; 4. what/who (though mocking is disrespectful no matter who the person); 5. what (omission); 6. why; 7. where; 8. what; 9. what; 10 why; 11. why; 12. who; 13. what; 14. why; 15. how. You and your students may come up with even better answers. Try to have a reason for them, though.

*Step 4:* (Optional) You may wish to show a short film here to help students apply what they have learned thus far.

A good one on the theme of competition is *Winning* (see A-V section). Also, *Cipher in the Snow* is a dramatically moving film about the death of a high school student known by hardly anyone.

By introducing a film here you will have another case to carry along through the rest of the chapter for the sake of discussion and application of the reality-revealing questions.

*Step 5:* Introduce the concept of *Think,* that is, consideration of alternatives and consequences. You can do this by sharing with students the examples discussed in the text. You may wish to elaborate on a number of these. Any number of the cases treated in the text could stimulate extended case discussions.

   a. Another way to examine alternatives and consequences is to discuss the newspaper articles introduced in Step 2.

   b. Discuss the exercise on p. 43 and the two exercises on p. 47.

   c. A good way to look at alternatives and consequences is through a film treating the mechanization of modern man like *Homo Homini* or the situation of a teen unwed mother depicted in *I'll Never Get Her Back.*

*Step 6:* Here are a couple of possibilities for treating the *Others* part of the STOP sign, pp. 47-49.

a. Have students make a log of a given day of their lives. In 15-minute segments, have them list what they do and which people they encounter. Share these. Discuss how it is virtually impossible to do anything without affecting other people in some way. Make the point that moral actions affect others in the same way.

b. Assign students the task of discussing the lifeboat case and one other case with at least four other people. Include in the assignment: parents, a peer who is not taking the course and another person they greatly respect. Have students give a short report on what their respondents said and what they themselves learned from the assignment.

c. (Optional) Show the film *Helen Keller* or *No Man Is an Island* to stress how related we are to other people, how much we affect them (and they us), how much we depend on others.

d. (Optional) A good resource to know about is Richard Reichert, *Simulation Games for Religious Education* (Winona, Minnesota: St. Mary's College Press, 1975). Reichert has a number of nice little simulations that could help illustrate the need for others. Especially good here are "Nonsense Syllable" (p. 28) and "Senses Walk" (p. 51).

e. Discuss exercise on p. 28 of Reichert's book.

*Step 7:* One of the most effective ways to present *Prayer* as an element in the moral decision-making process is to give *personal,* heartfelt testimony on how the Lord helped you make key decisions in your life. You might even tell your students the frustrations of teaching religion but how prayer is invaluable in giving you the strength and courage to carry on. You can also share with students why you teach religion, how you feel it is a real calling, a vocation.

a. Answer any questions students have about the text material and the four methods of prayer mentioned there: praying together; meditation; reflection on events in life; the assurance that prayer will be answered.

b. It is very important to give students some concrete examples of prayer. To this end you may try one of the following:

   (1) Have students keep a journal during the course. The theme of the journal should be how God works in one's life through ordinary events and people encountered each day.

   (2) Each class should begin with prayer (perhaps spontaneous prayer), where the teacher (or others) puts students consciously in the Lord's presence and asks for his guidance and strength to see his Father's will manifested in the topic under discussion.

   (3) Guide the students in a meditation. Betsy Caprio's *Experiments in Prayer* and *Experiments in Growth* (Notre Dame: Ave Maria Press, 1973, 1976) are outstanding resources. Her guided meditations on getting to know Jesus from *Experiments* (pp. 106-132) are fantastic. Richard J. Hulesman, S.J., *Pray* (New York: Paulist Press, 1976) also contains a number of helpful ideas that can be adapted to the high school classroom. Finally, Sr. Bernadette Vetter, H.M., *My Journey, My Prayer* (New York: Wm. H. Sadlier, Inc., 1977) has its feet on the ground when it comes to practical ideas for prayer for high

school students. I have found all of these very useful.

(4) Select a theme like power, prestige, or sex. Have students find scriptural passages on that theme that will help them reflect on a New Testament approach to the issue. Pose a case on the theme like the one on money discussed on p. 49 of the text and solicit student insights on how scripture addresses the issue. This would be a good small-group discussion topic.

*Step 8:* Review the Summary to the chapter and apply the S-T-O-P of the STOP sign to the case at the end of the chapter. This case is based on the short film *It's My Hobby.* This is an excellent film and has provided my classes with some stimulating discussions.

## SUGGESTED AUDIOVISUAL IDEAS

*Cipher in the Snow* (24 min. color film; Brigham Young University). A high school student dies because of rejection and loneliness. A sensitive and provocative film about caring and loving. (Step 4)

*Helen Keller* (15 min. color film; McGraw-Hill). Shows how the concern of one person has lasting results in contributing to forming one of the world's great women. (Step 6)

*Homo Homini* (11 min. color animated film; Mass Media Ministries). Shows what happens if mankind becomes too mechanized. Human values transcend mere machinery. (Step 5)

*I'll Never Get Her Back* (24 min. black and white film; National Film Board of Canada). What is it like to be an unmarried teenage mother? A true story showing the agony of a young person giving up her baby for adoption. (Step 5)

*It's My Hobby* (11 min. color film; CRM Educational Films). Thematically the same as the case at the end of the chapter. The conflict is between social responsibility and personal loyalty. Excellent discussion starter. Also helpful in identifying Kohlberg stages. (Step 8)

*No Man Is an Island* (11 min. color film; Dana Productions). Orson Welles narrates John Donne's poem with a collage of pictures in the background stressing the theme that the quality of our life affects others. (Step 6)

*Winning* (16 min. color film; Time-Life). Mike Wallace narrates a segment on the philosophy behind competition in amateur sports. (Step 4)

## TIME USED

Class 1: Step 1 and Step 2a
Class 2: Step 2b and c
Class 3: Step 3
Class 4: Step 5a and b
Class 5: Step 6
Class 6: Step 7
Class 7: Step 8

*Additional classes:* add one class each if you use: Step 4, Step 5c, Step 6c or d.

## ADAPTATION FOR CCD CLASSES

If at all possible, try to show *It's My Hobby*. Use this as a basis for developing the various elements of the S-T-O-P.
*Step 1:* (15 min.) Using the basic approach the process described in Step 2b of the procedure outlined above, search out the 5 *w's* and *h* in selected news articles. While doing this, share with students some of the insights from the *Search* material on pp. 28-37.

*Step 2:* (10 min.) Explain the two principles of Catholic morality discussed on p. 37 and p. 39.

*Step 3:* (10 min.) Discuss the exercises on p. 38 and p. 40.

*Step 4:* (10 min.) Discuss alternatives and consequences in light of the exercises on pp. 43 and 46.

*Step 5:* (15 min.) After briefly explaining the role of considering and consulting others as well as prayer, spend the rest of the class applying STOP to the case at the end of the chapter.

*Alternative:* Give a brief lecture on the S-T-O-P part of the STOP sign, illustrating by way of examples in the text. Show *It's My Hobby* (11 min.) or a suitable substitute and then discuss in light of the brief lecture given.

# 3

# The STOP Sign, Continued

## BACKGROUND

This chapter continues the explanation of the STOP sign method of moral decision-making. There is a logical connection between the elements discussed in the previous chapter and those treated in this chapter. The connection is prayer which puts one in contact with Jesus. Jesus himself is seen as the norm of Christian morality we are called to follow. His life and teaching help us to put our own moral decisions into context. This takes the form of a couple of serious questions which ask whether what we propose to do is loving and if it is in the service of others. Answering these two questions can go a long way to helping a person sift out the complexities involved in moral action.

Under the themes of reason and revelation the notion that moral action is equivalent to *human* action is treated. Reason attunes us to natural law which is extremely helpful in determining the human thing to do in a given situation. Revelation helps unveil a true human identity and helps us realize one's dignity and worth. These two concepts help disclose a Christian concept of the human person. Many helpful insights on how we should live the dignity of personhood that we possess flow from this concept.

Imagination is introduced to stress that creative insight can be very helpful in resolving difficult moral issues. Although the STOP sign method does place heavy emphasis on a person's rational faculties, it also sees the importance for intuitive insight and imagination.

Finally, this chapter discusses the very helpful role of the objective norm in morality, namely, law. Law is defined according to the valuable insights of Thomas Aquinas. Then, a clear distinction is made between various kinds of law: natural law, civil law, divine law and church law. Under this topic, there is an extended treatment of the Ten Commandments and the Beatitudes. Teachers of Christian morality ought to expect their students to know these and especially the values each of them tries to preserve.

## FURTHER READING FOR THE TEACHER

Abata, C.SS.R., Russell. *You and the Ten Commandments: A Series.* Liguori, Mo.: Liguori Publications, 1976, 1977. A series of helpful little pamphlets any number of which could be nice supplementary reading for students.

Barclay, William. *The Ten Commandments for Today.* Grand Rapids, Michigan: Wm. B. Eerdmans Publishing Co., 1973. Some fresh insights on the Commandments from the renowned Protestant biblical scholar. His historical background on the Commandments is especially illuminating.

Curran, Charles E. *Themes in Fundamental Moral Theology.* Notre Dame: University of Notre Dame Press, 1977. A collection of some of Curran's best essays. The first essay on "The Relevance of the Gospel Ethic" is highly recommended reading. Also helpful are his second essay on natural law and his third on church law. Curran at his best.

Gillon, O.P., Louis B. *Christ and Moral Theology.* Staten Island, N.Y.: Alba House, 1967. Shows the relevance of Aquinas to contemporary morality's search for answers. A tightly written, helpful book.

Haring, C.SS.R., Bernard. *Toward a Christian Moral Theology.* Notre Dame: University of Notre Dame Press, 1966. An easily read book that will give good background to teaching this chapter. Chapters 4, 5, 7, 9 and 10 are highly recommended.

Lohkamp, O.F.M., Nicholas. *The Ten Commandments and the New Morality.* Cincinnati: St. Anthony Messenger Press, 1973. A popular book that stresses the positive in morality. Good student reading, too.

Macquarrie, John. *Three Issues in Ethics.* New York: Harper & Row, Publishers, 1970. Chapter 4 on natural law is outstanding and must reading. Macquarrie is a highly respected Protestant theologian.

Middleton, Jr., Carl L. and Robert P. Craig. *Teaching the Ten Commandments.* West Mystic, Conn.: Twenty-Third Publications, 1977. An extremely valuable book for teachers. You will find in it many helpful activities to implement with your students. Highly recommended.

O'Grady, John F. *Christian Anthropology.* New York: Paulist Press, 1976. An outstanding primer on the Christian understanding of the human person. Excellent bibliographies are provided at the end of the book.

Schnackenburg, Rudolf. *The Moral Teaching of the New Testament.* New York: Herder and Herder, 1966. The *classic* in New Testament ethics.

Spurrier, William A. *Natural Law and the Ethics of Love.* Philadelphia: The Westminister Press, 1974. Spurrier reflects on the differences between classical Catholic and Protestant approaches to morality. You may not agree with all of his conclusions, but he does have some good syntheses. Also, you will like how he attempts to tackle some difficult issues in morality in Chapter 6.

## OBJECTIVES

That the student . . .

1. *Characterize* the ethical teaching of Jesus.

2. *Define* the meaning of agape-love.

3. *Evaluate* one's own attitude toward money.

4. *Characterize* a Christian definition of human person.

5. *Apply* the elements in a Christian definition of the human person to concrete moral situations.

6. *Appreciate* the role of imagination in moral decision-making.

7. *Define* law and recognize different kinds of law.

8. *Know* the Ten Commandments and the Beatitudes and *explain* the values inherent in each of them.

## PROCEDURE

*Step 1:* Distribute to each student a copy of the New Testament. Students are to study the Sermon on the Mount (Mt 5-7) to get a sense of the ethical teaching of Jesus. Break them into at least three groups (perhaps six groups). Each group is to be responsible for a given section of the Sermon. A convenient breakdown is Chapter 5, 6 and 7. Each group should be prepared to give a brief summary of what is in that section. In your synthesis of the Sermon, highlight the following points:

*Chapter 5:*

a. The Beatitudes: no need to cover these here as they appear later in the chapter under "Law."

b. How can a teenager be light of the world? Salt of the earth?

c. Jesus came to fulfill the law.

d. The six antitheses: Jesus' law of love contrasted with the old law:

| *Old* | *New* |
|---|---|
| 1. No killing. | 1. No anger. |
| 2. No adultery. | 2. No lust. |
| 3. A writ for divorce. | 3. No divorce. |
| 4. No oath-breaking. | 4. No oath-taking. |
| 5. "Eye for eye." | 5. Turn the other cheek. |
| 6. Love neighbor, hate enemy. | 6. Love even the enemy. |

*Chapter 6:*

a. Purity of intention: Jesus looks to the motive.

b. Three works expected of Christians:

(1) Almsgiving: do it without fanfare
(2) Prayer: the Our Father and simplicity
(3) Fasting: what is the value of fasting for contemporary Americans? What about eating junk food?

c. Confidence in God.

*Chapter 7:*

a. Avoid judgment: how does this apply to the high school student?

b. Power of prayer

c. The Golden Rule

If your students are open to it, you might have each group write a little skit and act it out to illustrate one of the themes of the Sermon. Have them contemporize the theme in the style of some of the skits in *Godspell*.

*Step 2:* Summarize the material on pp. 57-63. Have students do the exercises on pp. 64-65.

*Step 3:* Write the following statements on the board or the overhead:

> a. "Those who expect to reap the blessings of freedom must . . . undergo the fatigue of supporting it." (Paine)

> b. "It is the best of times, it is the worst of times." (adaptation of Dickens)

> c. "The people's good is the highest law." (Cicero)

> d. "The wave of the future is coming and there is no fighting it." (A.M. Lindbergh)

> e. "The only thing necessary for the triumph of evil is for good men to do nothing." (Burke)

Have students rank-order these as to which one states best the current situation of humanity.

Ask them these questions: What philosophy of life does each person who uttered a given statement probably have? Where do we get our philosophy of life, our concept of what is good for the human person? (reason and revelation)

*Step 4:* Draw a stick figure of a human on the board. Around it list the various traits of the human person discussed on pp. 67-73. Spend a few moments explaining each along the lines described in the text.

(Optional) Should you wish to stress one or another of these points, you may wish to do so by way of a film. *What Are We Doing to Our World?* is good for stewardship, man's sinfulness, beings with a history, and with and for others, etc. Any environmental kind of film integrates a number of these points well. *Cosmic Zoom* is an outstanding film to show how humans fit into the cosmic scheme of things.

*Step 5:* Spend some time on the exercises on pp. 73-74.

*Step 6:* If at all possible, show the film *Why Man Creates* to get at the themes discussed on pp. 74-76. If this is impossible, share some insights from this section with your students. Have them discuss in light of this section the cases on p. 77.

*Step 7: Law*

a. Share with students Aquinas' definition of good law on pp. 78-80. It might be good to analyze school rules in light of the four points discussed on pp. 79-80.

b. Differentiate between the four kinds of law discussed on pp. 80-84. Ask students to produce examples of their own for each of these.

c. Spend some time on the Ten Commandments and the Beatitudes and the values each tries to preserve. Students should be accountable for knowing these by heart.

d. Do the exercises on pp. 85-86.

*Step 8: Summary*

a. Summarize the chapter.

b. Have students briefly write out an answer to the case on p. 87 before discussing it as a large group.

(Optional) This might be a good time to discuss drinking and drugs. These tie into the reason/revelation section of the chapter. The film *Alcoholism: Out of the Shadows* might be a good way to get into the topic. As you know, drug abuse is a major moral issue for high school students. It is worth introducing the topic here and then once again in Chapter 8 by way of a case.

## SUGGESTED AUDIOVISUAL IDEAS

*Alcohol—A Dilemma for Youth* (2 filmstrips, 20 minutes; General Board of Education, Methodist Church). Acquaints teens with the complexity of the alcohol problem and the relations of decisions about alcohol to a young person's total personality and life. (Step 4 or 8)

*Alcoholism: Out of the Shadows* (30 min. color film; Xerox Corporation). A good film on alcoholism. Shows the dangers of alcohol abuse, its effects, ways to ask for help and the like. (Step 4 or 8)

*Buttercup* (11 min. color film; Teleketics). A poetic meditation beautifully filmed. Shows how living things depend on one another. (Step 4)

*Chromophobia* (11 min. color film; International Film Bureau). An animated film that helps one realize the responsibility we have towards others. Stresses the various aspects of conformity and loss of uniqueness. (Step 4)

*Cosmic Zoom* (11 min. color film; McGraw-Hill Book Co.). Blends live photography and animation into a fascinating exploration of life. Depicts man in proper perspective in relation to both macroscopic and microscopic universes. (Step 4)

*Matthew 5:5* (5 min. color film; Teleketics). Encourages us to see ourselves in the light of the Beatitudes as people of promise, waiting to inherit the earth. (Step 1 or 7)

*What Are We Doing to Our World?* (27 min. color film; McGraw-Hill). The narrator is Walter Cronkite. The film raises ethical, aesthetic and moral considerations about lack of concern for the environment. (Step 4)

*Why Man Creates* (25 min. color film; Pyramid Films). An excellent film which explores the nature of creativity and how creativity happens. Stresses the fact that creativity involves natural gifts, hard work and patience. (Step 6)

## TIME USED

    Class 1: Step 1
    Class 2: Step 1 and Step 2
    Class 3: Step 3 and Step 4
    Class 4: Step 4
    Class 5: Step 5 and Step 6
    Class 6: Step 7
    Class 7: Step 8

*Optional classes:* Add a class if you show a film in Step 4 or the ones recommended in Step 8.

## ADAPTATION FOR CCD CLASSES

There is a lot of material in this chapter. Thus, I suggest a quick overview and then work from the exercises.

*Step 1:* (20 min.) Give an overview of the main points in each of the sections under Jesus, Revelation and Reason, Imagination and Law.

*Step 2:* (10 min.) Apply all of the overview elements to the lifeboat case and ask some of the questions in the sections which treat the case.

*Step 3:* (30 min.) Discuss the following exercises.

  a. Exercise 2 on p. 64;

  b. Exercise 3, pp. 73-74;

  c. Case on p. 77.

  d. Case on pp. 87.

  e. If time remains, do exercise 1 on p. 85.

# 4

# The STOP Sign, Concluded

## BACKGROUND

Chapter 4 concludes the study of the moral decision-making process known as the STOP sign. Four elements are treated to round off the discussion: church, values, instinct and conscience. The church is presented as a rich source of moral guidance for Catholics. After a brief discussion on the source of the church's authority to teach in areas of morality, the chapter shows where church teaching in moral matters can be found both in its formal presentations and in the more informal ways with which most Catholics are familiar. Fellow believers are stressed as an important source of counsel and spiritual aid in doing the right thing.

Under the topic of values the notion that many moral issues involving a conflict of values is introduced. Students are alerted to the valuing process and are informed that a possible solution to moral issues can be had by ranking conflicting values. A good number of exercises are provided for students to clarify their own values on important moral issues.

The notion of moral imperative is treated under the term instinct. Students are told that sometimes "gut-level" reactions to moral issues can be an initial trustworthy guide to choosing the right thing. Feelings are not to be ignored in seeking the right thing to do. They must be listened to, thought about and measured against other elements in the STOP sign. Sometimes they can be very helpful in making moral decisions.

The chapter concludes with a presentation on conscience and two important principles concerning it: namely, conscience must be followed and it must be continuously formed and informed. Several definitions of conscience are provided.

Chapter 4 concludes with a couple of relevant cases. The first deals with shoplifting, the second with personal authenticity.

An important element in teaching this chapter is to bring in continuously the other elements of the STOP sign with which students are already familiar. This will reinforce what they have learned and also help them remember it.

## FURTHER READING FOR THE TEACHER

Bockle, Franz and Jacques-Marie Pohier. *Moral Formation and Christianity*. Concilium, No. 110. New York: The Seabury Press, 1978. Helmut Juros has a perceptive article on the formation of conscience. Kevin Ryan has a short critique on moral formation in America.

Burtchaell, C.S.C., James Tunstead. *Philemon's Problem: The Daily Dilemma of the Christian*. Chicago: ACTA, 1973. This book is must reading to really appreciate *Christian* morality. Excellent background reading to this entire course.

Chervin, Ronda. *The Art of Choosing*. Liguori, Missouri: Liguori Publications, 1975. This work-study book has a number of helpful questions that could be of great assistance in teaching this chapter and the book, too. It is a rich book.

Deedy, John. *What a Modern Catholic Believes about Conscience, Freedom & Authority*. Chicago: The Thomas More Press, 1972. A popularly written little book, Deedy raises some interesting questions about conscience in conflict with authority. May give you several cases for discussion.

Harrington, O.F.M., Jeremy, ed. *Conscience in Today's World*. Cincinnati: St. Anthony Messenger Press, 1970. The first three articles are excellent supplementary reading for students on the topic of conscience.

Hauerwas, Stanley. *Vision & Virtue*. Notre Dame, Indiana: Fides Publishers, Inc., 1974. The second essay broadens moral vision beyond mere rational analysis. Hauerwas knows how to do ethics.

Nelson, C. Ellis, ed. *Conscience: Theological and Psychological Perspective*. New York: Paulist Press, 1973. Perhaps the best collection of topflight essays on the topic of conscience.

O'Connell, Timothy E. *Principles for a Catholic Morality*. New York: The Seabury Press, 1978. I highly recommend this book for a basic introduction to Catholic moral theology. It is recent and it is good.

Ryan, Mary Perkins, ed. *Toward Moral Maturity*. New York: Paulist Press, 1968. Some of the essays in this little classic are still very helpful. O'Neill's essay concluding the book is good background for this chapter.

Sloyan, Gerard S. *How Do I Know I Am Doing Right?* New York: Cebco Pflaum, 1976. A marvelous little book on how to make moral decisions in a Christian context.

## OBJECTIVES

That the student . . .

1. *Recognize* how the church can be a source of guidance in moral decision-making.

2. *Know* the church's commandments.

3. *Apply* the value-clarifying process to selected moral situations.

4. *Appreciate* the role instinct has to play in moral decision-making.

5. *Define* conscience and articulate two principles connected with it.

6. *Evaluate* a couple of moral cases in light of the entire STOP sign method of moral decision-making.

PROCEDURE

*Step 1:* Summarize the material on the church on pp. 89-94. Ask for questions on this material.

a. Go through the laws of the church found on pp. 93-94. Discuss them in light of the exercise on p. 94 (#2).

b. Discuss exercise #1 on p. 94.

*Step 2:* I highly recommend that a long-term assignment in this course is to require each student to research a topic in the area of morality for a report later on in the course. This would be an excellent place to introduce the assignment. The rationale for the assignment is simple: each student should be able—by the end of the course—to begin answering questions about specific moral issues, or at least know where to go for an answer. Furthermore, it is important that students be able to find a "Catholic" position on the topic as well. To this end, here are some ideas:

a. Spend a class explaining how to do basic research by way of articles and books. It can be very helpful for students to learn how to research an article from *The Catholic Periodical and Literature Index.* This valuable aid indexes a number of important topics found in the most popular journals. Make a list of

Catholic periodicals found in your school library or local library to facilitate their research.

b. Give students a few hints on how to interview. A part of the research project can be to talk directly to "experts" in a given field of morality: parents, teachers, priests, professors, those in the medical profession and the like. Stress the gathering of facts: answering what, why, who, where, when, how.

c. Make students responsible for reporting the information they gather in a systematic way. A traditional approach is a short (say five page) term paper with an oral presentation. (If you opt for this, plan to allow five-six days for student reports and sharing.) An alternative is a taped talk which presents the "meat" of the research. At the least, students should have note cards for each resource. A minimum expectation would be around five resources, three of which ought to come from "Catholic" sources. Many ideas for topics are sprinkled throughout the student text.

*Step 3:* Values.

a. Summarize the material on pp. 94-97.

b. Spend some time on the exercises on pp. 97-101. This is an important section for teaching the notions of clarifying and ranking values in conflict situations. Students often enjoy sharing their coat of arms, exercise #6, p. 101.

*Step 4:* Discuss the ideas presented in the section on "Instinct," pp. 102-104. Have students make a list of actions that elicit initial moral outrage. The text suggests a few of these like cloning and increased spending for nuclear weapons.

*Step 5:* A good way to cover the topic of conscience is by way of a film. Here I recommend three outstanding film clips from Learning Corporation of America.

They are *Authority and Rebellion* from Herman Wouk's *The Caine Mutiny; A Matter of Conscience* based on Robert Bolt's *A Man for All Seasons;* and *Pride and Principle* from *The Bridge Over the River Kwai.* In your discussion of the film, be sure to stress:

- the two principles of conscience: Form it and follow it.

- the three aspects of conscience as stressed on pp. 106-107.

*Step 6:* Summary. Do the exercises that end the chapter. Have students share their responses.

(Optional) When I teach conscience, I stress the theme of authenticity, of being who we are. Students respond to this notion because of their great aversion to hypocrisy. An excellent filmstrip that shows how we hedge, how we cover up our true selves is John Powell's, S.J., *Why Am I Afraid to Tell You Who I Am?* based on his outstanding book by the same name. Students are very responsive to this filmstrip. It helps them see that moral action is greatly facilitated by good communication. You may well want to use his ideas here or elsewhere in the course, especially Chapter 5.

## SUGGESTED AUDIOVISUAL IDEAS

*An Arrow of Light* (15 min. color film; Biblical Cinema). Presents church as mystery concerned with social issues. Shows the presence of Christ in the church. Good background to church as presence of the Risen Lord. (Step 1)

*Authority and Rebellion* (28 min. color film; Learning Corporation of America). An edited version of *The Caine Mutiny* that shows a young naval officer who followed his conscience in following a rebellion against irresponsible authority. Excellent for a discussion of conscience. (Step 5)

*The Church Says but I Think* (2 filmstrips; 13 min. each; Thomas Klise Co.). The second filmstrip is valuable in showing how personal conscience grows in stages of awareness. (Step 5)

*Father/Daughter* (10 min. color film; Teleketics). A documentary that shows the conflict between the generations. Stresses communication, consequences of our actions and motivations behind individual life-styles. Good to show at the end of this chapter.

*Hangman* (12 min. color animated film; McGraw-Hill). Ogden Nash's classic poem illustrated. Stresses themes like the nature of prejudice and responsibility for our fellowman. Shows the importance an individual standing up for personal belief can have. (Step 5)

*A Matter of Conscience* (31 min. film; Learning Corporation of America). This is an outstanding film clip from *A Man for All Seasons*. Thomas More is presented as a Christian hero who is willing to die in order to do the right thing. Highly recommended. (Step 5) (This film is treated as a case in Chapter 9.)

*Pride and Principle* (17 min. color film; Learning Corporation of America). A snippet from *The Bridge Over the River Kwai*. It demonstrates the theme of living by principle, its motivation and its consequences as well as the question of the priority of values in a given situation. The scenario is a Japanese prison camp where two intransigent men meet and clash over a matter of principle, leaving in doubt the rightness of the victor's behavior. (Steps 3 and 5)

*Why Am I Afraid to Tell You Who I Am?* (2 filmstrips; 27 min.; Argus). An excellent filmstrip on the masks we hide behind in order to keep from revealing our true selves. Good on authenticity and open communication (supplementary).

TIME USED

>   Class 1: Step 1
>   Class 2: Step 2
>   Class 3: Step 3
>   Class 4: Steps 4 and 5
>   Class 5: Step 5
>   Class 6: Step 6

>   *Optional classes:* Add one class if you use Powell's material.

## ADAPTATION FOR CCD CLASSES

*Step 1:* (15 min.) Summarize the material on church and values, p. 89-96.

*Step 2:* (25 min.) Do exercise #2 on p. 98, exercises 4 and 5 on p. 99 and exercise 6 on p. 101. Share exercise #6.

*Step 3:* (10 min.) Give a short presentation on instinct and conscience as discussed in the text on pp. 102-107.

*Step 4:* (10 min.) Do either the first or second exercise at the end of the chapter.

# 5

# The STOP Sign Applied

## BACKGROUND

The purpose of this chapter is to take a relevant moral issue and analyze it in light of the STOP sign. Any number of issues could have been selected but sexual morality seemed appropriate because of high student interest in the topic. Besides, students are really looking for guidelines and the STOP sign can be of great help in establishing those guidelines. Each element discussed in the previous three chapters is applied to the issue. As a teacher, you are encouraged to add as many other insights to the discussion as you think necessary. The issue is a difficult one to confine to one chapter, so the discussion in the text had to be limited to some key points.

Perhaps the most important thing for you to do is to stress both the introduction to the chapter and the summary points on pp. 144-145. When confronted with the ideal of chastity and purity, students often feel a great deal of guilt because they have difficulty living up to the ideal. It is true that our young people must be encouraged to try to live the

56

ideal we Christians are called to incorporate in our lives. But it is also true that we are pilgrim people on our way, people who will fall from time to time in our attempts to follow the Lord. These failures should not be presented as "guilt trips" but rather as experiences of growth, experiences that can lead to healthful integration and steps toward wholesomeness. Jesus understands our sexuality and stands ready to forgive and offer his strength and help to his brothers and sisters on their journey to his Father. Thus, issues in premarital sexuality should be presented delicately and sensitively so that students are given the opportunity to grow in a caring, understanding environment.

Special features of the chapter include exercises designed to get students to question contemporary attitudes toward sex, to reflect on their attitudes to their own sexuality, to seek guidance from trusted adults and to question the double standard that seems to be very prevalent in views toward sexuality.

## FURTHER READING FOR THE TEACHER

Abata, C.SS.R., Russell. *Sexual Morality: Guidelines for Today's Catholic.* Liguori, Mo.: Liguori Publications, 1975. A popularly written pamphlet for high school students. Good supplementary reading for them.

*An American Catholic Catechism.* New York: The Seabury Press, 1975. Pp. 246-258 give a clear overview of sexual morality. Well done by balanced theologians.

Bockle, Franz and Jacques-Marie Pohier. *Sexuality in Contemporary Catholicism.* New York: The Seabury Press, 1976. Concilium, No. 100. Some good critical essays on human sexuality. Breuning's article on responsible sexuality as an educational goal is especially relevant for teachers.

Curran, Charles E. *Contemporary Problems in Moral Theology.* Notre Dame, Indiana: Fides Publishers, Inc., 1970. His essay on sexuality and sin is timely reading.

*Declaration on Certain Questions Concerning Sexual Ethics.* Rome: Sacred Congregation for the Doctrine of Faith (January 22, 1976). The latest official statement of the church relating the traditional teaching in the area of sexual morality.

Dedek, John. *Contemporary Sexual Morality.* New York: Sheed & Ward, 1971. Good background reading. Typically clear and lucid.

Greeley, Andrew. *Sexual Intimacy.* Chicago: Thomas More, 1973. Written with Greeley's typical wit and charm. Some beautiful chapters.

*Human Sexuality: New Directions in American Catholic Thought.* A Study Commissioned by the Catholic Theological Society of America. New York: Paulist Press, 1977. This is the controversial book produced in the '70s on human sexuality. There are a number of valuable insights. The bibliography is outstanding.

May, William E. and John Harvey. *On Understanding Human Sexuality.* Chicago: Franciscan Herald Press, 1977. A critical review of the Catholic Theological Society's *Human Sexuality.*

O'Neil, Robert P. and Michael A. Donovan. *Sexuality & Moral Responsibility.* Washington: Corpus Books, 1968. Good psychological perspectives on sexuality.

Taylor, S.J., Michael J., ed. *Sex: Thoughts for Contemporary Christians.* Garden City, New York: Image Books, 1973. A good collection of articles. Dominian's article on pornography is quite good.

Trobisch, Walter. *Love Is a Feeling to Be Learned.* Downers Grove, Illinois: Inter-Varsity Press, 1971. A short book good for student reading.

Woods, O.P., Richard. *Another Kind of Love: Homosexuality and Spirituality.* Chicago: Thomas More, 1977. A sensitive discussion of homosexuality.

## OBJECTIVES

That the student . . .

1. *Apply* the STOP sign method of moral decision-making to premarital sexual morality.

2. *Analyze* some contemporary views of human sexuality.

3. *Clarify* one's own attitude toward his or her sexuality.

4. *Reflect* on possible sources of guidance in the area of sexual morality.

5. *Articulate* clearly the church's stand on premarital sexuality.

6. *Appreciate* the support, understanding and guidance the Christian community offers to young people in their growth toward sexual integration.

## PROCEDURE

*Preliminary:* Ask students to read the entire chapter first before you begin discussing it in class. They need not fill in the exercises yet, but they should have some idea of the theme of the chapter. Ask them to write down any questions that might occur to them as they read. These questions will be turned in anonymously so that you can have a question-answer session with your students.

*Step 1:* As a class project, write on the board the 5 w's and h discussed on pp. 111-114. Have students answer these questions. Write their various responses on the board. Supplement their answers with material in the text. Draw some of the same conclusions as are treated on p. 115. Do the exercise on p. 116.

*Step 2:* Share with students material from pp. 116-119. Ask for their reaction to the television talk show example on p. 117. Do the exercise on p. 119.

*Step 3:* Invite to class a young married couple or even parents of some of the students to discuss their reactions to the problem of "sexploitation" in American society. Tie in as part of this discussion the material on others and prayer, pp. 120-122.

*Step 4:* Carefully stress the positive aspects of Jesus' teaching, pp. 123-124, and make sure students understand the reason and revelation section, pp. 125-128. This is in many ways the key section of the chapter and should be treated carefully. Share exercises on p. 131 and pp. 135-136.

*Optional but highly recommended:*
Show and discuss in detail the films *To Be a Man* and *To Be a Woman.* Solicit student reactions to the stereotypes treated therein.

*Step 5:* Make sure students understand the imagination and law sections. Discuss questions on p. 129 and p. 130.

*Step 6:* It would be good to read in class and comment on each of the points under the topic of Church, pp. 130-132. Do exercises on p. 132.

*Step 7:* After treating "instinct" and "conscience" on pp. 133-134, have students write a response to dilemmas on p. 134.

*Step 8:* Summary. Allow time for a question-answer session prepared for by students anonymously writing out their questions.

## SUGGESTED AUDIOVISUAL IDEAS

*Man and Woman* (28 min. color film; Learning Corporation of America). This is a cutting from the film *The Taming of the Shrew.* It depicts "the battle of the sexes," dramatizes the conflict between men and women in their search for love, and provokes a discussion on "Women's Liberation." (Step 3)

*The Question* (10 min. color animated film; McGraw-Hill). A man searches for the meaning of life and pursues an answer by going to people who answer from the perspectives of a bishop, politician, mathematician, executive, psychiatrist and army officer. The answer he seeks is love. (Step 1)

*Remember Eden* (10 min. color film; Cine-Catholic). To the background of Vivaldi's "The Four Seasons," this film stresses the need for fidelity in man-woman relationships. A beautiful film. (Step 3)

*To Be a Man* (14 min. color film; Billy Budd Films). A collage of responses that help trigger the question of the meaning of masculinity. Helps young people better understand themselves. Good discussion starter. (Step 4)

*To Be a Person* (19 min. color film; Billy Budd Films). Helps define that to be a person means to be respected and to be loved. Stresses importance of communication of self and listening to others to get a good self-concept. (Step 2)

*To Be a Woman* (14 min. color film; Billy Budd Films). Young people are pictured trying to define the meaning of womanhood. Good companion film for *To Be a Man*. (Step 4)

*To Be in Love* (14 min. color film; Billy Budd Films). Gets at a definition of romantic love. Keys in on the problem of sex and its relationship to commitment. Good discussion starter. (Step 5)

## TIME USED

Class 1: Steps 1 and 2
Class 2: Step 3
Class 3: Step 4
Class 4: Steps 5 and 6
Class 5: Steps 7 and 8

*Extra class:* Add one class if you show the films in Step 4.

## ADAPTATION FOR CCD CLASSES

*Step 1:* (25 min.) Put the STOP sign on the board. Raise the issue of premarital sex and work through the various elements. Ask questions of students to inductively get at some of the major points raised in the chapter. Answer their questions as you go along.

*Step 2:* (10 min.) Do the exercise on p. 116.

*Step 3:* (10 min.) Do exercises # 4 and 5 on p. 119.

*Step 4:* (5 min.) Do the exercise on p. 128.

*Step 5:* (10 min.) Give students the choice of working on exercise #2, p. 132 or the two letters on p. 134. Share responses.

# 6

## Moral Pluralism

---

BACKGROUND

This chapter introduces the concept of moral pluralism, an important idea since students are bombarded by different philosophies of life in our society. These philosophies greatly influence how a person will decide moral issues in the practical order. The key notion you wish to get across is that various people come up with different answers on the same moral issue because they have different starting points—especially in regard to what they think the human thing is in a particular situation. Pluralism is a fact that students in our contemporary society have to live with; they need to understand the concept.

The vehicle for illustrating moral pluralism in this chapter is the controversial topic of abortion. Many other topics could have been selected to illustrate the point, topics like capital punishment, war, and technological advancement. But I believe abortion is the major moral tragedy of contemporary times. Regardless of what some people maintain, our students have not had their "fill" of this topic. We too often wrongly assume that they understand and have heard all the issues involved. My experience is that they have not. If

Catholics are to remain leaders in the area of life issues, it is extremely important that our young people know church teaching and are aware of the approaches of those who advocate abortion on demand. Time spent on this topic will reap benefits in years to come.

I offer only one caution in teaching this chapter. It goes without saying that Christians are more than a one-issue people. Abortion is not *the* only human life issue with which we are concerned. However, it does symbolize the callous attitude of many in contemporary society toward human life. The points on pp. 163-165 should be stressed to put the entire issue in proper perspective. Also, it is highly recommended that students be given the opportunity to involve themselves in some pro-life activity so that—as young people—they have the chance to affirm publicly their beliefs on these important issues. A couple of these activities are suggested on p. 165.

## FURTHER READING FOR THE TEACHER

The bibliography given at the end of the chapter in the student text contains many helpful references for the teacher. Included here are a few of the really good things available for teaching this topic to young people.

Dillon, Valerie V. *Nine Facts to Know About Abortion.* Washington, D.C.: NCCB Committee for Pro-Life Activities, 1974. This 16-page question and answer booklet treats medical, legal, biological and theological aspects of abortion. It costs 25¢ and would make good supplementary reading for students.

*Documentation on Abortion and the Right to Life,* Part I and Part II. Washington, D.C.: USCC Publications, 1975 and 1976. An excellent resource for teachers. Gives the testimony of American Catholic bishops before the Senate (1975) and House (1976) on a human life amendment to the Constitution.

Gaffney, James. *Moral Questions.* New York: Paulist Press, 1974. Has a nice chapter delineating the arguments on the abortion controversy (Chapter 3). This is a nice book that has several penetrating articles on various moral topics.

Granfield, David. *The Abortion Decision*. New York: Image Books, 1969. An excellent introduction to the topic. Easily available.

May, William E. *Human Existence, Medicine and Ethics*. Chicago: Franciscan Herald Press, 1977. Excellent argumentation throughout from a traditional perspective. Chapter 5 is on the abortion issue.

Milhaven, John Giles. *Toward a New Catholic Morality*. New York: Image Books, 1972. Contains many helpful articles on different moral issues. Chapter 5 lines up the arguments on abortion in a masterful way.

Williams, Mary Kay. *Abortion: A Collision of Rights*. National Catholic News Service. A 32-page booklet that serves its title well.

Willke, Dr. and Mrs. J. C. *How to Teach the Pro-Life Story*. Cincinnati: Hiltz & Hayes Publishing Co., Inc., 1973. Many good ideas for teachers.

## OBJECTIVES

That the student . . .

1. *Characterize* the concept of moral pluralism.
2. *Differentiate* between different philosophical stances on the abortion controversy.
3. *Recognize* the difference between fact and opinion on abortion.
4. *Analyze* the rhetoric behind different postions on abortion.
5. *Articulate* the Catholic position on pro-life issues, especially in regards to the issue of abortion.
6. *Take* a public stand on the abortion issue.

PROCEDURE

*Step 1:* Define for students the meaning of *pluralism,* that is, the societal condition which allows for a multiplicity of ways to approach reality. Because there are different operative principles, there will be different practical solutions to moral issues. Ask students to list and discuss evidences of pluralism in the following situations:

- American politics
- the Vietnam War
- sexual morality

Discuss the reasons for pluralism. Try to elicit responses that include some of the following:

- different ethnic groups
- different economic backgrounds
- different religious beliefs
- different perceptions of reality

*Step 2:* Role-play the Abortion Debate on pp. 140-143. Analyze the debate as suggested in the text, pp. 143-147.

*Step 3:* Pick other moral issues and have students write and enact a script modeled on the Abortion Debate. Assign six people to a group. Four students will enact the dialogue (they can create their own cast of characters); one will introduce the topic to the larger class; at the end of the debate, another will analyze the debate for the other groups.

Other possible topics: premarital sexual morality
war
capital punishment
more money for nuclear weapons
enforced school busing
euthanasia

*Step 4:* a. Discuss the question at the end of the Abortion Debate, p. 144.

b. Do the Fact vs. Opinion exercise on p. 144. For the sake of the exercise, define fact as that which is based on reality; opinion is a point of view that scientifically may be difficult to "prove beyond the shadow of a doubt." Good opinions are ultimately based on facts; bad opinions are erroneous. The "scientific mind" wants "facts" proven empirically. Statement 5 is empirically verifiable. Opinions to the empiricist cannot be verified scientifically. Although it may be difficult to convince an empiricist of the basis in fact of statements 1, 3, 4 and probably 7, we ought to stress that in light of statement 5 these are at the least good opinions. The Catholic viewpoint would hold that statements 2, 6, 7 (abortion is *not contraceptive*), 9 and 10 are bad opinions.

c. Do the exercise on pp. 147-148. The answers would probably run thus: Johnson; Williams; Jones; Smith (although you could make a case that the last two are interchangeable).

*Step 5:* Present the Catholic teaching on abortion as outlined in the chapter, pp. 149-154. You can do this in a number of ways. Included below are some of these.

a. *The STOP sign approach.* Utilizing the bibliography at the end of the chapter, the text material, the teacher bibliography, articles from available Catholic periodicals, taped talks, etc., conduct an in-class research project. Create several learning stations around the classroom. Assign small groups to be responsible for researching various parts of the STOP sign. For example, one group could handle church teaching, another, imagination, instinct and values, still another, the *Search,* etc. For students, mark salient passages from the resources available. Allow a period or two for the research and another for reports to the larger class. Systematically outline the major points around a large STOP sign drawn on the board or on butcher paper posted on one wall of the room. To enhance the seriousness (and uniqueness of the project), you may want students to invite guests to class on the day of the report. Principals, parish priests, parents are likely candidates.

b. *Guest speaker.* Invite to class a speaker from a local pro-life organization. They are eager to come and share their programs and the rationale for them. Most all of them speak *gratis.*

c. *Films.* Show several of the excellent films or filmstrips annotated below. Supplement with discussion.

*Step 6:* Summary and action project. It is very valuable for young people to get involved in this issue. There are a couple of ideas on p. 154. I have tried both with great success.

## SUGGESTED AUDIOVISUAL IDEAS

The suggested placement for showing these is Step 5 above.

*Abortion: A Woman's Decision* (22 min. color film; ACTA). An unwed high school girl is faced with the dilemma of accepting responsibility for her pregnancy. She contemplates abortion; her father agrees. Her mother wants a talk with the family doctor to take place first. The doctor explains the issue clearly to the girl and concludes that it is still her decision. Helps develop the idea that a "real person" is one who chooses what is best for self *and* others.

*The Beginning of Life* (26 min. color film; Pyramid). Shows the actual process of conception and earliest stages of life—from cell formation to the first heartbeat of the human embryo.

*Birthday* (7 min. color film; San Francisco Archdiocesan Communications Center). Shows the actual thought processes of a woman who decides to give birth rather than have an abortion.

*Choose Life* (56 frame color filmstrip; Ikonographics). Shows why abortion is detrimental to the social community.

*The Committee* (12 min. color film; ACTA). A futuristic film depicting a select group that plays God in decisions of life. Helps show that the same rationale that led to legalized abortion may lead to legalized euthanasia.

*The First Days of Life* (24 min. color film; For Life, Inc.). Depicts the humanity of the unborn child from the beginning of life through delivery. Shows that human life is indeed a continuum.

*Life Before Birth* (2 10 min. filmstrips; Time-Life). A valuable aid to the study of human conception, cell division and embryonic development through birth.

*Love and Let Live* (77 frame slide show; Michigan Catholic Conference). Shows the humanity of the unborn child, the destructiveness of abortion, the necessity of a constitutional amendment to protect unborn human life.

*A Life Too Brief* (10 min. color film; NCCB Pro-Life Committee). Same theme as *Love and Let Live*.

*Respect Life* (24 min. color film; W. A. Palmer Films, Inc.). Various segments showing pro-life attitudes beyond the prebirth stages.

## TIME USED

Class 1: Step 1
Class 2: Step 2
Class 3: Step 3
Class 4: Steps 3 and 4
Class 5: Step 4
Classes 5-8: depend on length of Step 5 and Step 6

## ADAPTATION FOR CCD CLASSES

*Step 1:* (20 min.) Role-play Abortion Debate, pp. 140-143. Debrief along lines of pp. 145-147. Discuss question on p. 144.

*Step 2:* (10 min.) Do Fact vs. Opinion exercise on p. 144.

*Step 3:* (5 min.) Do exercise on pp. 147-148.

*Step 4:* (25 min.) Using the STOP sign method and supplying needed information as you go along, discuss with students the following case. Use some of the material on pp. 149-154.

"A girl friend of yours has told you she is getting an abortion. She has gotten pregnant recently and just 'knows' that her parents will disown her if they ever find out. Her 'boyfriend' doesn't care one way or another if she aborts. What would you advise her and why?"

# 7

# Morality and Sin

## BACKGROUND

This chapter treats the concept of sin. Sin is presented as more than just a mistake in judgment or miscalculation. One problem in teaching a method for making moral decisions might be to let students think that evil is involved in our actions only because we somehow failed to follow through on the ethical method. This may sometimes be true. But there is more to sin than making mistakes. St. Paul best describes the reality of sin in *Romans* when he says that he fails to do what he wants to do, but does that which he hates. Sin is all over our lives—it is a reality one cannot escape due not only to personal malice but also to the sinful condition into which we are all born (original sin).

The chapter begins with a survey on sin in order to elicit student attitudes towards it. This can be used as a pre-test to see what should be emphasized in the rest of the chapter. Biblical images of sin as "missing the mark" and "hardness of heart" are related to the notion of the seven capital sins, sins of omission and sins of commission. Exercises are presented so that students become more aware of these categories.

After this introduction, the key idea of sin as a negative response to God's love is treated. Here, God is pictured not as an ogre who waits for us to sin but rather as a loving Father who stands ready always to forgive his children when they fall. There is a discussion of the different degrees of sin—mortal, serious and venial. Exercises are provided to help teach this section.

The chapter ends with the topic of Jesus and the forgiveness he offers through the sacrament of Reconciliation. You may very well want to provide for a celebration of this sacrament to conclude the chapter.

## FURTHER READING FOR THE TEACHER

Bausch, William J. *It Is the Lord!* Notre Dame, Indiana: Fides Publishers, Inc., 1970. This is a beautiful little book on sin and confession. Very positive and pastoral in tone.

Bockle, Franz. *The Manipulated Man.* New York: Herder and Herder, 1971. Shows another side to sin—namely, manipulation used in societal structures and institutions.

Foley, Leonard. *Your Confession: Using the New Ritual.* Cincinnati: St. Anthony Messenger Press, 1975. An excellent book on the new rite. It contains a great survey on recent developments on the theology of sin. Very readable. Recommended for student use, too.

Haring, Bernard. *Sin in the Secular Age.* Garden City, New York: Doubleday & Co., Inc., 1974. Many helpful insights on sin in the contemporary world. Up to Haring's high standards.

Kennedy, Eugene. *A Sense of Life, A Sense of Sin.* Garden City, New York: Image Books, 1976. A pleasant book with some helpful psychological insights. Stresses personal responsibility.

Maly, Eugene H. *Sin: Biblical Perspectives.* Dayton: Pflaum/Standard, 1973. An excellent book on the topic and highly readable, too.

Menninger, Karl. *Whatever Became of Sin?* New York: Hawthorn Books, Inc., 1973. Argues convincingly for a rediscovery of the concept of sin for a healthy approach to reality.

Monden, Louis. *Sin, Liberty and Law*. New York: Sheed & Ward, 1965. Monden's distinctions are classic and helpful to teachers.

Sawyer, S.S.N.D., Kieran. *Developing Faith: Lesson Plans for Senior High Religion Classes*. Notre Dame, Indiana: Ave Maria Press, 1978. An excellent resource. Her chapter on sin and reconciliation will give you many ideas to help teach this chapter.

Scanlan, Michael. *Inner Healing*. New York: Paulist Press, 1967. An excellent and inspiring book showing the roots of our alienation from God and how to begin to cope with the change necessary to grow closer to him.

Schoonenberg, S.J., Piet. *Man and Sin: A Theological View*. Notre Dame: University of Notre Dame Press, 1965. Theology at its best. A key work on the topic of sin.

Shea, John. *What a Modern Catholic Believes about Sin*. Chicago: Thomas More, 1971. Engagingly written with many fresh insights.

Van der Poel, Cornelius J. *The Search for Human Values*. New York: Paulist Press, 1968. The new approach to morality at its best. Sin presented as antihuman.

## OBJECTIVES

That the student . . .

1. *Investigate* his/her own attitude to sin.
2. *Characterize* biblical dimensions of sin.
3. *Differentiate* between sins of omission and sins of commission.
4. *Recognize* different degrees of sin.
5. *Evaluate* certain characterizations of God.
6. *Appreciate* the role of Jesus and the forgiveness he offers.

## PROCEDURE

*Step 1: Introduction.* Have students write their own definitions of sin and list certain things they know for sure to be sinful for teenagers. Discuss these. Introduce the chapter by doing the exercise on pp. 160-161. Share this exercise.

*Step 2:* a. Briefly explain sin as "missing the mark" and "hardness of heart" as discussed on pp. 162-163.

b. In treating sins of omission, first define the term, and then have students analyze one day of their lives in 15-minute segments, perhaps the day prior to the one on which this class is held. Have them make a list of opportunities they missed where they could have been more loving, like greeting someone, being more helpful at home, spending time with a younger brother or sister. Share these if the students wish to do so.

c. Do the exercises on p. 165. Discuss.

*Step 3:* Present in short summary form the material on pp. 167-171. Spend the rest of the class discussing the exercises on pp. 171-173.

*Step 4: Witness* to the role of the sacrament of Reconciliation in your life. Include some of the comments from the chapter, pp. 173-174. Prepare with students a communal celebration of the sacrament. Divide students into groups and have each group work on a given task. Here are some ideas:

*Group 1:* Writes out an examination of conscience for young people. (Let them begin by looking at the Commandments, the Beatitudes and some of the exercises in the chapter.)

*Group 2:* Selects an appropriate "forgiveness" parable and prepares either a skit or dramatic reading of it. (Luke 15 is a good start for this project.)

*Group 3:* Selects a number of songs or background music to be played while the class is confessing.

*Group 4:* Prepares the service itself. Suggested outline:

1. An opening prayer.

2. A scripture reading and reflection presented by Group 4.

3. The "forgiveness" parable from Group 2.

4. Meditation on the examination of conscience by Group 1.

5. Confession of sin—background music and songs.

6. Closing prayer of thanksgiving.

*Step 5:* Penance service.

## SUGGESTED AUDIOVISUAL IDEAS

*A Man Had Two Sons* (7 min. color film; Boston Catholic Television Center). An updated version of *The Prodigal Son.* Might be nice to include in the penance service.

*Night and Fog* (31 min. color film; McGraw-Hill). This is a hard-hitting classic on Hitler's atrocities towards the Jews. Not for people with weak stomachs. But it is excellent to show the reality of sin. (Step 1)

*Parable* (22 min. color film; Cine-Catholic). This film has been around for a while and your students may have seen it. But if not, it is an excellent short Christ-allegory based on a circus clown. Also criticizes the evils of jealousy and violence in society. (Step 2, 3, or 5)

*Penance—Sacrament of Peace* (10 min. color film; Teleketics). A touching story of a man who hits a girl with his car while driving home from a party. He asks her forgiveness. Shows the need to express sorrow. (Step 4)

*The Stray* (14 min. color film; Teleketics). An allegory on the Parable of the Lost Sheep. A child gets lost at the zoo and the chaperone goes back to find him. A celebration follows. (Step 4)

## TIME USED

Class 1: Step 1
Class 2: Step 2
Class 3: Step 3
Class 4: Step 4
Class 5: Step 5

## ADAPTATION FOR CCD CLASSES

*Step 1:* (10 min.) Do the exercise on pp. 160-161. Discuss in light of the introduction to the chapter.

*Step 2:* (20 min.) Briefly explain the biblical concepts of sin and sin as omission and commission as treated on pp. 162-164. Do exercises on p. 165.

*Step 3:* (20 min.) After explaining the misconceptions of God (p. 167), briefly share with students the degrees of "saying no" as treated in the text. Do the exercises on pp. 171-173.

*Step 4:* (10 min.) Witness briefly on what the sacrament of Reconciliation has meant to you in your life. Ask students to share their own positive experiences as well.

# 8

# Solving Moral Problems: What About Life?

## BACKGROUND

This chapter begins the three-chapter treatment of moral problems, giving students the opportunity to apply what they have learned. The five cases in this chapter deal with life issues: life-saving courtesy while driving, the morality of smoking, euthanasia, capital punishment and alcoholism. Included in the chapter is an appendix with bibliographies for student research and a few theological notes on church teaching on euthanasia and capital punishment.

Special features of the chapter include a short orientation on the reasons why Christians should respect life, and a human life inventory that seeks to elicit student attitudes toward various life issues.

It is highly recommended that students do research on other life issues as suggested at the end of the chapter. These may well be taken as small group research projects.

# FURTHER READING FOR THE TEACHER

Please refer to the bibliographies in the student text. These should prove very helpful in teaching a couple of the topics included in the chapter. Here are some other helpful resources.

Beach, Waldo and H. Richard Niebuhr. *Christian Ethics.* New York: The Ronald Press Company, 1973. This second edition is a historical overview of Christian ethics through the ages. There is a strong emphasis on Protestant ethics in the second half of the survey. This is helpful to see how other Christians approach moral argument.

Curran, Charles E. *Blueprints for Moral Living.* Chicago: Claretian Publications, 1974. A nice readable overview of many moral issues. A very short treatment but Curran gets to the heart of the matter.

Douglass, James W. *The Non-Violent Cross: A Theology of Revolution and Peace.* London: Collier-Macmillan, Ltd., 1968. An excellent theology of war from the perspective of a leading pacifist.

Dyck, Arthur J. *On Human Care: An Introduction to Ethics.* Nashville: Abington, 1977. A good introduction to ethics, using examples from life issues.

Fletcher, Joseph. *Morals and Medicine.* Boston: Beacon Press, 1960. You won't agree with many of the conclusions of Fletcher, the modern-day advocate of situation ethics, but it is good to know his line of argumentation. This is his classic book on medical ethics.

Heyer, Robert, ed. *Medical/Moral Problems.* New York: Paulist Press, 1976. Pithy essays on medical ethics. An overview essay by Curran, an article on the mentally retarded, an essay on the ethics of transplants are especially helpful.

Marty, Martin E. and Dean G. Peerman, eds. *New Theology No. 10: The Ethical and Theological Issues Raised by Recent Developments in the Life Sciences.* New York: The Macmillan Company, 1973. An excellent collection of essays from many different perspectives.

Ramsey, Paul. *Fabricated Man.* New Haven: Yale University Press, 1970. An excellent book by one of the leading Christian moralists. Some stimulating arguments on the ethics of genetic control.

## OBJECTIVES

That the student . . .

1. *Articulate* the reasons for the Christian's respect for life.
2. *Examine* one's own attitudes to various life issues.
3. *Evaluate* selected cases on the theme of life in light of the STOP sign.
4. *Differentiate* between active and passive euthanasia and ordinary and extraordinary means.
5. *Recognize* the church's teaching on capital punishment.
6. *Research* a human life issue.

## PROCEDURE

*Step 1: Opening exercise.* On the board, have the class contrast two different philosophies of life, that of a hedonist (Playboy) and that of a mature Christian. How would they answer each of these questions?

*Hedonist*                                                    *Christian*

What is our purpose in life?

What is the successful life?

What is the value of money?

How should the sexes relate?

What role should others play in our life?

What is the meaning of sacrifice?

Discuss these contrasts.

(Optional) Assign short research projects for home-work from topics listed at the end of the chapter.

*Step 2:* Have students read the first part of the chapter, pp. 177-179. Discuss with them.

*Step 3:* Have students fill in the human life inventory, pp. 179-180. Share and discuss.

*Step 4:* Discuss Case #1 in a large group, pp. 180-182. In light of the discussion in Step 1, how would a hedonist solve this problem?

*Step 5:* Have each student work on Case #2 (pp. 182-183) individually. Share results in a large discussion.

*Step 6:* Read through Case #3, pp. 184-185. Clarify the material in the appendix, pp. 189-193. Discuss questions at the end of the case in small groups. Share with rest of the class.

*Step 7:* Have materials handy for the debate in Case #4, pp. 185-186. Allow students to work on assembling arguments either pro or con. Have a debate on the issue. Point out weak arguments as well as church teaching on the issue. Discuss case #5.

*Step 8:* If you had students researching their own issues during the past few days, allow time for short reports at the end of this unit.

## SUGGESTED AUDIOVISUAL IDEAS

Some of these can be used to supplement the cases in the chapter or to provide original case material for discussion.

*But Jack Was a Good Driver* (15 min. color film; CRM Educational Films). Raises the question about a friend's possible suicide. Helps gain an understanding of the clues to potential suicide and how best to act when suicide appears a possibility.

*Chickamauga* (33 min. black and white film; McGraw-Hill). A war is enacted in the imagination of a little boy. Shows the devastation of war.

*The Garden Party* (24 min. color film A.C.I. Films). A family preparing for a party hears of the death of a neighbor. The daughter is sent to comfort the family and for the first time experiences death. A good stimulant for the discussion of death.

*Gift of Life* (20 min. color film; Pyramid Films). Against the backdrop of scripture readings, life in its various ages is wonderfully depicted. Shows that the Bible is applicable to everyday living not just to the best and worst moments in life.

*Living with Dying* (two 30 min. filmstrips; Sunburst Communications). A visual presentation of Elisabeth Kubler-Ross' theories on the stages a person may go through as he approaches the inevitability of death.

*The Price of Life* (12 min. color film; Paulist Productions). Three short vignettes on various topics: morality of war, abortion, an elderly retarded man and friendship. Good discussion starters.

*Though I Walk Through the Valley* (30 min. color film; Pyramid Films). Documents the last six months in the life of Tony Brouwer, a Christian husband and father with terminal cancer. Helps to see the witness of a man of faith and courage in the face of death.

*Violence Just for Fun* (15 min. color film; Learning Corporation of America). A film snippet from the feature film *Barabbas*. Shows Roman spectators applauding gladiators as they destroy other humans. Raises the whole question on the tradition of violence in entertainment.

## TIME USED

Class 1: Steps 1, 2 and 3
Class 2: Step 4
Class 3: Step 5
Class 4: Step 6
Class 5: Step 7
Class 6: Step 8

*Extra class:* Add a class if you show a film or two.

## ADAPTATION FOR CCD CLASSES

*Step 1:* (10 min.) Have students read the introduction to the chapter, pp. 177-179. Ask for questions and discuss, if necessary.

*Step 2:* (10 min.) Do the human life inventory, pp. 179-180. Share and discuss.

*Step 3:* (40 min.) Discuss two of the five cases presented. *Alternative:* Break class into five small groups. Have each work on a different case and reach consensus on it. Then allow each group five minutes to make a short presentation to the other students.

# 9

# Solving Moral Problems:
# Truth and Justice

## BACKGROUND

Like Chapter 8, Chapter 9 contains a number of cases related to a given theme, specifically truth and justice issues. This is an important area of study for two reasons: (1) Truthfulness is an issue that is of much concern to young people. On the one hand, they admittedly have a difficult time with hypocrisy in any form; but, on the other hand, cheating is generally a serious problem in our schools. (2) Justice is a theme that must be treated in any moral problems text lest students think all morality is just personal morality. This is a good place to bring into focus social issues and provide the opportunity for students to apply what they have learned to the larger community.

The chapter begins with a couple of rank-order exercises on truth and justice. Next, honesty is defined and its merits discussed. This is followed by a justice survey, a discussion of the distinction between various kinds of justice, a situation for discussion, a short summary of church teaching on justice and a listing of practical things a concerned Christian can do. The chapter also includes five cases for extended discussion. One of these latter cases provides an opportunity to discuss specific recommendations made by Pope Paul VI in his famous encyclical *Populorum Progressio*.

A bibliography is provided for further student research. It is highly recommended that you require students to read some of the church teaching found in the social documents. The chapter ends with a list of several activities for direct student involvement in social issues. If students have not yet participated in either some kind of research project or an action project in this course, Chapter 9 provides one of the final opportunities for them to do so.

## FURTHER READING FOR THE TEACHER

You will find the student bibliography contained in this chapter of the text helpful to you in teaching the chapter. Please refer to it and also the titles of the church documents on social teaching. These few works listed below are also very good.

Fenton, Thomas P. *Education for Justice: A Resource Manual*. Maryknoll, New York: Orbis Books, 1975. A fantastic teacher resource book on justice. Section 3 on educational designs gives many practical strategies, including workable simulation games. Should prove invaluable.

Gallagher, Mal, J. B. McGinnis, *et al. Educating for Peace and Justice: A Manual for Teachers*. St. Louis Institute for the Study of Peace, St. Louis University, 1974. An exhaustive collection of current peace education literature on all grade levels. Methodology is process and person oriented.

Hesburgh, C.S.C., Theodore M. *The Humane Imperative*. Yale University Press, 1975. A series of lectures on the meaning of the gospel for the future of society. Does not reject capitalism but sees it can be reformed with the injection of lived Christian principles.

*Justice in the World.* A secondary-level course developed by the Division for Justice and Peace of the United States Catholic Conference, Washington, D.C. There are seven modules: 1. Church and the World. 2. A Global View. 3. Three Worlds. 4. American Dilemma. 5. The Right to Develop. 6. American Power. 7. Charity/Justice.

Mainelli, Vincent, ed. *Social Justice: The Catholic Position.* Consortium Press, 1975. Includes complete texts of Catholic social teaching.

Mische, Gerald and Patricia. *Toward a Human World Order.* New York: Paulist Press, 1977. Offers concrete strategies on how concerned people can work for grass-roots changes in social structures.

Neal, S.N.D. de N., Marie Augusta. *A Socio-Theology of Letting Go.* New York: Paulist Press, 1977. Some interesting insights on the nature of relinquishment.

Ryan, William. *Blaming the Victim.* New York: Vintage Press, 1972. Shows how we blame the victims of poverty rather than the real villain, the inequality of American society.

Schrank, Jeffrey. *Teaching Human Beings: 101 Subversive Activities for the Classroom.* Boston: Beacon Press, 1972. Contains scores of teachable activities to sensitize students to different issues. Highly recommended. Also, see his *The Seed Catalogue: A Guide to Teaching/ Learning Materials* (Boston: Beacon Press, 1974) for hundreds of resources for the classroom teacher. Both of these books should be in your library.

Shumacher, E. F. *Small Is Beautiful.* New York: Harper and Row. Shows an alternative to the mega-economics of today. Some useful insights.

OBJECTIVES

That the student . . .

1. *Examine* his/her attitude on a number of justice issues.
2. *Appreciate* the role of honesty in character development.
3. *Distinguish* among different kinds of justice.
4. *Articulate* several points of church teaching on social justice.
5. *Analyze* and *evaluate* several justice/honesty issues.
6. *Research* an issue in social justice.

PROCEDURE

*Step 1:* Have students do the exercises on pp. 198-199. Discuss them.

*Step 2:* Have students read pp. 199-200 on honesty. Ask for their reactions to the material contained therein. Do the justice survey on pp. 200-201. Share responses.

*Step 3:* Conduct a simulation game to teach the concept of justice. "Global Village" from the Maryknoll Global Education Program is especially effective. Class is divided into proportions representing the major divisions of haves and have-nots:

¾ represents underdeveloped world
¼ represents affluent world (¼ of these represent USA and Canada)

Distribute the resources of soft drinks and paper cups according to the following scale:

½ to USA and Canada
¼ to affluent world (Europe)
¼ to underdeveloped world

Further sophistication can be added by apportioning the soft drink (raw materials) and the cups (capital goods) so that the group representing Europe gets a few more cups than their supply of soft drink.

Students can trade thus: 1 soft drink=3 cups. Instruct them to trade for their needs. (If folding chairs are available, they can be used to represent living space and mobility: 1 chair=1 soft drink=3 chairs.)

Make notes while activity ensues. Stop when a "revolution" (stealing) begins to take place. Get student reaction to the exercise.

Debrief by defining terms on pp. 201-203.

Other possible games for this step:

1. "The Coffee Game," Thomas Fenton. The Christophers, 12 East 48th Street, New York, New York 10017. Shows the economic imperialism toward Latin America.

2. "Baldicer," Georgeann Wilcoxson. John Knox Press, Box 1176, Richmond, Va. 23209. A simulation of the dynamics of food production, technology, population growth. Time: 2 hours with debriefing.

*Step 4:* Read and discuss cases on p. 203.

*Step 5:* Present church teaching by way of an audiovisual resource, listed below. Discuss and supplement with material on pp. 204-206.

*Step 6:* Discuss cases on pp. 207-211.

*Step 7:* Summarize and assign one of the projects suggested at the end of the chapter.

## SUGGESTED AUDIOVISUAL IDEAS

Any number of these could be shown in Step 5 above to initiate a discussion of church teaching.

*Agenda for the '70s* (20 min. filmstrip; U.S. Catholic Conference). Points up current social problems in America today. Shows the need America has for churches to interest themselves in social action programs.

*All Doctrine Is Social Doctrine* (15 min. filmstrip; Thomas S. Klise Co.). Gives a general introduction to social gospel—the implications of faith for contemporary social and economic orders. Beatitude morality is pictured as public morality.

*Come to Life* (11 min. color film; Teleketics). Seen through the eyes of a small child, the viewer pictures a documentary of American life and is led to see that Christians have the responsibility to share with less fortunate people.

*Contact* (10 min. color film; Teleketics). Dramatizes the social, economic, and educational conditions of the urban indigents and migrant workers. Helps to promote a deeper sense of social involvement on a personal and church level.

*Crime and Criminal* (28 min. black and white film; Learning Corporation of America). A snippet from the famous movie *In Cold Blood*. Raises the question to what extent society should allow understanding of the criminal's motivations to influence its laws and its sense of justice. Good for a discussion of capital punishment, too.

*A Day in the Night of Jonathan Mole* (32 min. black and white film; McGraw-Hill). A dream fantasy about a man who is cast as a judge of an Indian, a Jew and an immigrant who aspire to higher employment positions. His ruling fits the law of the land—a place for everyone and everyone in his place. Good on the theme of prejudice, too.

*Despite Man's Differences* (20 min. color film; McGraw-Hill). Examines causes of segregation and prejudice throughout history. A balanced presentation.

*Flavio* (12 min. black and white film; McGraw-Hill). A sad film about the mass starvation in the world. Shows how the human spirit endures the worst odds, and moves the Christian spirit to feel for the poor, the hungry and the diseased.

*Glass House* (12 min. color film; Teleketics). A highly allegorized film where a rich man isolates himself from the poor. His "middle class" servant perpetuates the myth of isolation by telling the poor they "have to make it." Good in showing that not only the rich, but also the middle class, perpetuate the oppression of the "have-nots."

*Land of the Brave* (8 min. color film; Teleketics). Dispels the stereotypes of the poor as "lazy" and "uncaring"; instead reveals the spiritual strength and physical courage of the 34 million Americans who live in poverty.

*Race and the Christian* (15 min. filmstrip; Thomas S. Klise Company). Shows the position the Christian should take regarding racism.

*Tilt* (19 min. color film; CRM films). In animation, three methods of sharing the world's wealth are discussed: "God helps those who help themselves"; "Casting bread upon the waters"; and "Two heads are better than one." Humorous but telling on the theme of wealth-sharing.

*Whether to Tell the Truth* (18 min. color film; Learning Corporation of America). A film clip from *On the Waterfront*. A young man has to decide whether to testify about a murder regardless of the personal consequences for him. Great on the theme of honesty.

## TIME USED

Class 1: Step 1 and Step 2
Class 2: Step 3
Class 3: Step 4
Class 4: Step 5
Classes 5-6: Step 6
Class 7: Step 7

## ADAPTATION FOR CCD CLASSES

*Step 1:* (15 min.) Do the exercise on pp. 198-199 .

*Step 2:* (10 min.) Do the justice survey, pp. 199-200.

*Step 3:* (10 min.) Summarize the kinds of justice described on pp. 201-203. Work on one of the two exercises on p. 203.

*Step 4:* (15 min.) Read in class the church teaching on pp. 204-206. Clarify if need be.

*Step 5:* (10 min.) Discuss one of the cases at the end of the chapter.

# 10

## Reasoning Morally and Conclusion

### BACKGROUND

Chapter 10 concludes the text by introducing the work of Lawrence Kohlberg and his insights on moral development. His six stages of moral reasoning help students see the various levels of moral thought and are useful in order to clarify the cognitive framework out of which individuals make moral decisions. Kohlberg is not to be "canonized" in this chapter but merely presented as an important thinker in the area of moral education who helps us get a better picture of how people sometimes arrive at moral decisions.

There is a section in this chapter that discusses moral heroism—the call of Christians. What often keeps individuals from choosing the heroic thing is conformity. Students are challenged to look at the reasons why we conform and are asked to evaluate their own tendencies to conform by means of a "Conformity IQ" continuum. This chapter also includes several more cases where students have the opportunity to apply the Kohlberg material as well as the STOP sign.

A short self-check quiz that covers the main points of the chapter is provided. You may wish to use this quiz as a post-test to enable you to evaluate what sections of the text need further development or review.

## FURTHER READING FOR THE TEACHER

Blatt, Colby, and Speicher. "Hypothetical Dilemmas for Use in Moral Discussions," Moral Education Research Foundation, 1975. Some practical strategies for classroom use.

Galbraith, Ronald and Thomas Jones. "Teaching Strategies for Moral Dilemmas," *Social Education,* January, 1975, pp. 16-22. Some good ideas for implementing Kohlberg materials.

McBride, Alfred. "Moral Education and the Kohlberg Thesis," *Momentum,* December, 1973, pp. 23-34. Written with McBride's typical lucidity.

Pagliuso, Susan. *Understanding Stages of Moral Development: A Programmed Learning Workbook.* New York: Paulist Press, 1976. Taking the time to work through this book will give you a basic familiarity with Kohlberg's stages.

Traviss, Sister Mary Peter. "Moral Education in the Classroom," *The Catechist,* March, 1976. Sr. Mary Peter is a leader in the field of moral education and role playing.

Wilson, John. *Ideals.* New York: Morehouse-Barlow Co., Inc., 1972. Subtitled "A Guide to Moral and Metaphysical Outlooks," this is a mind-expanding book on different approaches to morality. Highly recommended.

Wilson, John. *Moral Education and the Curriculum.* Oxford: Pergamon Press, 1969. Some useful ideas included in this book on how to structure curricula.

## OBJECTIVES

That the student . . .

1. *List* and *discuss* reasons for conformity in moral decision-making.

2. *Differentiate* between the six stages of moral reasoning.

3. *Evaluate* himself/herself on a conformity continuum.

4. *Analyze* and *discuss* several cases in light of the STOP sign and Kohlberg's six stages.

5. *Self-evaluate* his/her understanding of the major points of the text.

## PROCEDURE

*Step 1:* Summarize Kohlberg material on pp. 219-222. Elicit student reaction to the material on moral heroism, p. 222.

*Step 2:* Do the exercises on p. 223. Discuss questions at end.

*Step 3:* Assign two cases from pp. 224-225 to small groups. Each group should reach consensus and report back to the entire class.

*Step 4:* Allow each student a full period to take the quiz. Correct.

*Step 5:* Review key points as dictated by results of the quiz.

## SUGGESTED AUDIOVISUAL IDEAS

*The Good, Good Life* (11 min. color film; Teleketics). A satiric film which explores the nature of advertising. An older man resists his family's attempts for him to get meaning out of things. (Step 3)

*Moral Development* (28 min. color film; CRM Films). A dramatic reenactment of Milgram's research with a discussion of Kohlberg. Excellent. (Step 1)

*The Prejudice Film* (28 min. color film; Motivational Media). Narrated by David Hartman, this is an outstanding film on prejudice. (Step 3)

*Up Front* (28 min. color film; Aims Instructional Media). A documentary on drug abuse. Rehabilitated drug addicts discuss the problems and solutions to drug abuse. (Step 3)

*A Time for Decision* (27 min. color film; Hollywood Film Enterprises). Shows alcoholism as a sickness that calls for medical, psychological and spiritual attention. These last two films make students aware of rehabilitation programs available to victims.

## TIME USED

Class 1: Step 1
Class 2: Step 2 and Step 3
Class 3: Step 3
Class 4: Step 4
Class 5: Step 5

## ADAPTATION FOR CCD CLASSES

*Step 1:* (20 min.) Summarize Kohlberg material. Do exercises on p. 223.

*Step 2:* (15 min.) Talk about the concept of moral heroism. Elicit student reaction.

*Step 3:* (10 min.) Discuss one of the cases at the end of the chapter.

*Step 4:* (15 min.) Select a sampling of the questions and quiz the class as a group.

## ADDRESSES FOR FILMS AND FILMSTRIPS

A C I Films Inc.
35 West 45th Street
New York, New York 10036

ACTA Foundation
4848 N. Clark Street
Chicago, Illinois 60640

Aims Instructional Media
P.O. Box 1010
Hollywood, California 90028

Alpha Corporation of
  America
1421 Armour Blvd.
Mundelein, Illinois 60060

Argus Communications
7440 Natchez Ave.
Niles, Illinois 60648

Biblical Cinema
1404 W. Wisconsin Ave.
Milwaukee, Wisconsin 53233

Billy Budd Films
235 E. 57th Street
New York, New York 10022

BNA Communications Inc.
9401 Decoverly Hall Rd.
Rockville, Maryland 20850

Boston Catholic Television
  Center
Box 56
55 Chapel Street
Newton, Massachusetts
  02160

Brigham Young University
Media Marketing
W. 170 Stad.
Provo, Utah 84602

CBS, Inc.
51 W. 52nd Street
New York, New York 10019

Cine Catholic
371 5th Street
Manistee, Michigan 49660

CRM Educational Films
110 15th St.
Del Mar, California 92014

Dana Productions
6249 Babcock Ave.
North Hollywood, California
  91606

Films Incorporated
Div. of Public Media, Inc.
1144 Wilmette Ave.
Wilmette, Illinois 60091

For Life, Inc.
1917 Xerxes Ave.
Minneapolis, Minnesota
  55411

Hollywood Film Enterprises
6060 Sunset Blvd.
Hollywood, California 90028

Ikonographics, Inc.
P.O. Box 4454
Louisville, Kentucky 40204

International Film Bureau
332 S. Michigan Ave.
Chicago, Illinois 60604

Thomas S. Klise Company
P.O. Box 3418
Peoria, Illinois 61614

Learning Corporation of
America
711 5th Ave.
New York, New York 10022

Mass Media Ministries
2116 N. Charles Ave.
Baltimore, Maryland 21218

McGraw-Hill Book Co.
P.O. Box 404
Highstown, New Jersey
08520

Michigan Catholic
Conference
P.O. Box 157
Lansing, Michigan 48901

Motivational Media
8271 Melrose, Suite 204
Los Angeles, California
90046

National Film Board of
Canada
680 Fifth Ave.
New York, New York 10019

National Conference of
Catholic Bishops Pro-Life
Committee
1312 Massachusetts Ave.,
N.W.
Washington, D.C. 20005

W.A. Palmer Films, Inc.
611 Howard Street
San Francisco, California
94105

Paulist Productions
P.O. Box 1057
Pacific Palisades, California
90272

Pyramid Films
Box 1048
Santa Monica, California
90406

San Francisco Archdiocesan
Communications Center
50 Oak Street
San Francisco, California
94102

Sunburst Communications
Pound Ridge, New York
10576

Teleketics
Franciscan Communications
Center
1229 S. Santee Street
Los Angeles, California
90015

Time-Life
Time and Life Building
Rockefeller Center
New York, New York 10020

Xerox Films
XEROX Educational Center
1250 Fairwood Ave.
Columbus, Ohio 43216